FOCUSING OUR FAITH

Brethren in Christ Core Values

Evangel Publishing House
Nappanee, Indiana

Toll-free Order Line: (800) 253-9315 (7:30 a.m. to 4:30 p.m. EST)
Internet Website: www.evangelpublishing.com

Biblical quotations, unless otherwise noted, are from the New Revised Standard Version Bible, copyright 1989, by the Division of Christian Education of the National Council of the Churches of Christ in the USA, and are used by permission.

Cover Design: Ted Ferguson

ISBN: 1-928915-10-8

LCCN: 00-105460

Printed in the United States of America

0 1 2 3 4 5 EP 5 4 3 2 1

Contents

Contributors

Charles M. (Chuck) **Anderson** is the church planting pastor of the LaGrange Project (Brethren in Christ) in LaGrange, Ga. Before assuming his present position, he served as founding pastor of the Grace Community Brethren in Christ Church in Lawrenceville, Ga.

Harriet Sider Bicksler is editor of *Shalom! A Journal for the Practice of Reconciliation*, a quarterly Brethren in Christ publication on peace and social concerns. Residing in Mechanicsburg, Pa., she also serves as chair of Mennonite Central Committee U.S.

Terry L. Brensinger is chair of the Biblical and Religious Studies Department and Professor of Biblical Studies at Messiah College in Grantham, Pa. He previously pastored Brethren in Christ congregations in Kentucky and New York City, and has taught in Israel, Kenya, and Zambia.

David L. Hall is Senior Pastor of the Elizabethtown Brethren in Christ Church in Elizabethtown, Pa. He previously served on the pastoral staff of the Grantham Brethren in Christ Church in Grantham, Pa.

Luke K. Keefer is Professor of Church History at Ashland Theological Seminary in Ashland, Ohio. Before coming to Ashland, he taught at Messiah College in Grantham, Pa. He has served on numerous denominational boards.

Paul Lehman-Schletewitz, son of a church planting couple, serves as pastor of the Walnut Valley Brethren in Christ Church in Walnut, Calif. He is a member of the Pacific Conference Board for Brotherhood Concerns and a representative to Mennonite Central Committee West Coast.

Jay E. McDermond is Associate Professor of Christian Ministries at Messiah College in Grantham, Pa. He previously pastored the Nappanee Brethren in Christ Church in Nappanee, Ind. He has also taught in both England and Kenya.

Craig E. Sider serves as bishop of the Atlantic Conference of the Brethren in Christ Church. Prior to assuming this position, he pastored the Upper Oaks Brethren in Christ Church in Oakville, Ontario, Canada.

Harvey R. Sider pastored Brethren in Christ congregations in Cheapside, Toronto, and Stayner, Ontario, Canada. He has also served as a missionary in India, president of Niagara Christian College, bishop of the Canadian Conference, and as moderator of the denomination. Now retired, he works as a volunteer for the Canadian Conference.

Esther Spurrier served from 1975-1987 with Brethren in Christ World Missions in Zambia. She currently volunteers for both Brethren in Christ World Missions and New Hope Ministries, a local interchurch social service agency in Dillsburg, Pa.

Dwight W. Thomas is the Minister of Music at the Elizabethtown Brethren in Christ Church in Elizabethtown, Pa. He has also taught in the Music Department at Messiah College in Grantham, Pa.

John R. Yeatts is Professor of the Psychology of Religion at Messiah College in Grantham, Pa. He previously pastored the Fairland Brethren in Christ Church in Cleona, Pa, chaired the denomination's Board for Media Ministries, and served on the Board for Christian Education.

Introduction

by Terry L. Brensinger

Every Christian organization, as well as its leadership,
needs to bring out, dust off, discuss, refine, develop, display,
and implement its predominant values if it desires to make
significant spiritual impact in the twenty-first century.[1]
—Aubrey Malphurs

A few months ago, one of my colleagues at the college spoke with me soon after reading a paper that one of his students had submitted for class. In the paper, the student had clearly articulated and vigorously defended his position on the examined topic. While my colleague readily admitted that he disagreed with virtually everything that the student believed, he nevertheless could not contain his enthusiasm about the paper. "It's exciting," he proclaimed, "to finally encounter a person who really believes something!"

Oftentimes, it seems that people today do not believe much of anything. The world around us appears to be either intimidated, confused, or disinterested. For the intimidated, to announce a deeply held conviction would be to risk criticism and even rejection. For the confused, to hold an important belief verges on the impossible, given the vast array of seemingly conflicting ideas and values. Finally, for the disinterested, beliefs and convictions are personal and relative; people can believe whatever they want as long as they leave each other alone.

In such a world, the church is called to model and proclaim the wonderful message of Jesus Christ. Yet we at times also find ourselves intimidated, confused, and even disinterested, failing to announce clearly those things that are most important to us. As a result, our otherwise inspiring message loses its luster and fails to capture the imaginations of our listeners. After hearing an apparently uneventful sermon one day, for example, Goethe reportedly said to the inexperienced preacher, "Young man, it is certainties I need. I have doubts enough of my own."[2] With this in mind, what is it that we in the Brethren in Christ Church value?

Tracing our Roots

Throughout the years since its inception in the late eighteenth century, the Brethren in Christ Church has typically been described using three different labels; labels which have to some extent lost their meaning for many people in the contemporary world. According to these labels, the Brethren in Christ are Anabaptists, Pietists and Wesleyans.

Anabaptists

We trace our roots to various groups of Christians in sixteenth-century Europe who, though having much in common with major Protestant reformers like Martin Luther and John Calvin, sought to go further in restoring the church as they saw it portrayed in the New Testament. These Christians, called Anabaptists ("rebaptizers") by their opponents, accepted the Bible as the sole foundation for the church and sought to follow its teachings quite literally in every area of life. For example, they stressed that baptism was reserved only for adults who could freely and consciously confess faith in Christ, and they subsequently "rebaptized" people who had been baptized as infants. In addition, the Anabaptists emphasized the separation of church and state, believed that the church was called to model visibly the kingdom of God in the world, worked hard at developing genuine Christian community, and practiced pacifism or peacemaking.

Pietists

We also owe a portion of our identity to certain German believers who, in the seventeenth century, rejected the overly intellectualized expression of the Christian faith that had become popular within certain segments of the church. Without abandoning pursuits of the mind, these "Pietists" emphasized an intimate or experiential faith that went beyond the mere acceptance of correct doctrine. The Christian faith is a relationship with God, and it should not simply be affirmed with the head, but enjoyed with the heart.

Wesleyans

Finally, the Brethren in Christ have been deeply influenced by the teachings of the eighteenth-century British scholar and preacher, John Wesley. While recognizing the sinfulness and helplessness of human beings, Wesley and his followers emphasized the significant transformation that Christian conversion involves. They taught that believers in Christ could be freed from their bondage to sin and empowered by the Holy Spirit to live lives of holiness and obedience. The Christian life, therefore, is intended to be one of victory rather than an endless cycle of defeats.

The ideas and practices of these three groups of Christians—Anabaptists, Pietists and Wesleyans—have greatly shaped the Brethren in Christ Church down through the years. In all of our churches, influences from one or all of these traditions can be seen during any given gathering. Yet, once again, the labels have lost some of their meaning for many in the modern world. As the Brethren in Christ Church seeks to plant new congregations and nurture its members, contemporary categories are needed. Therefore, without discarding the older labels or downplaying their significance, the time has come for us to state in clear and accessible terms those convictions that are most dear to us as a church.

Stating Our Values

On May 6-8, 1999, 51 persons from throughout the Brethren in Christ Church in North America met to identify and restate those "core values" which most deeply resonate within our hearts and minds. These persons represented all levels and geographical areas of the church. In preparation for the meeting, all participants read *Reflections on a Heritage*, a recent compilation of Brethren in Christ identity statements.[3] Papers were presented, and discussion groups met throughout the gathering. Lively conversations even continued during mealtimes as men and women wrestled with the questions and issues facing us. Who are the Brethren in Christ? What are our most central beliefs and values? How can we articulate these beliefs and values in words that everyone can understand? At the end of the three days and a lot of spirited and prayerful give-and-take, these ten core values emerged:

- We value the free gift of salvation in Christ Jesus and the transforming power of the Holy Spirit.

- We value the Bible as God's authoritative Word, study it together, and build our lives on its truth.

- We value heartfelt worship that is God-honoring, Spirit-directed, and life-changing.

- We value wholehearted obedience to Christ Jesus through the empowering presence of the Holy Spirit.

- We value integrity in relationships and mutual accountability in an atmosphere of grace, love, and acceptance.

- We value an active and loving witness for Christ to all people.

- We value serving others at their point of need, following the example of our Lord Jesus.

- We value all human life and promote forgiveness, understanding, reconciliation, and nonviolent resolution of conflict.

- We value uncluttered lives, which free us to love boldly, give generously, and serve joyfully.

- We confess our dependence on God for everything, and seek to deepen our intimacy with him by living prayerfully.

These are our core values. These constitute our deepest and most central convictions. We have brought them out, dusted them off, discussed them, refined them, developed and displayed them. In an intimidated, confused and disinterested world, we believe that these core values are vitally important and worth standing up for. With God's help and for his glory, we also believe they are worth implementing!

In the following chapters, these core values are carefully examined and explored. In addition to discussing many of the relevant biblical passages, each writer shares stories, experiences, and discussion questions that help place these values within their contemporary contexts. Through this format, we hope that the book will serve as a valuable resource, not only for personal study, but also for Sunday school classes, small group meetings, family devotions, and other such gatherings. We further hope that you, the readers, will seek both to understand the meaning of each value as well as consider fresh and insightful ways of enacting them in today's world.

1

Experiencing God's Love and Grace

We value the free gift of salvation in Christ Jesus and the transforming power of the Holy Spirit.

by Luke L. Keefer, Jr.

Grace means there is nothing we can do to make God love us more...and...there is nothing we can do to make God love us less.... Grace means that God already loves us as much as an infinite God can possibly love.[1]
–Philip Yancey

As we drove to the hot dog stand near Messiah College, my roommate turned on the radio. A local station that we disliked and ordinarily avoided came on the air. Before we could tune in to another station, however, a voice interrupted the music for a special announcement. A five-year-old girl had wandered from her home in the mountains north of Harrisburg, Pennsylvania. Her mother last saw her playing in the yard about three o'clock in the afternoon. As it was now past eight o'clock on this dark and chilly evening in late fall, an urgent appeal came for volunteers to assist in a search.

My roommate and I returned to our dorm and rounded up two carloads of students to join the effort. We reached the location just as a new party was being organized to search the mountain above the house where the girl's family lived. The ten of us joined a line of about a hundred people, positioned so that our flashlights could cover the space between us and the person to our right and left. We moved up the mountain, checking everything along the way.

During a rest break, we students gathered and decided to pray that the girl would be found. The leaders of our search party were told by the command post near the house that the search would be called off until daylight. Some of the volunteers started back to their cars. Our leaders asked those who remained to spread out over an abandoned field that was in the process of returning to mountain land. We would cover this area as we worked our way back to the house. The command to proceed was passed along the search line and we started down the slope. After surveying no more than a hundred yards, a cry went up from a man two places to my right: "Here she is, and she's okay!" Quickly, people began running to the point of discovery.

In notifying the command post of the good news, our leaders requested that a jeep be sent up the mountain road to bring the girl down to her house. Fire sirens sounded to alert the thousand or more searchers in parties fanned out in all directions that the search was over. Our triumphant party followed the jeep on its slow descent to the house.

When we reached the public road and turned in the direction of the girl's house, we marched in a virtual processional. Rescuers lined both sides of the road. As the jeep made its way between them, people cheered and cried, empty coffee cups were thrown into the air, car horns honked, and sirens blew. The girl was returned to the safety of her parents' arms while everyone else went wild with joy.

Thirty-eight years later, as I write these lines, tears flow from my eyes as readily as they did that night. The search for the missing girl taught me the meaning of Jesus' words that heaven celebrates when one of God's lost children is found and returned to the safety of the Father's care (Luke 15:7). On that night, I sensed within my soul what it means to experience God's love and grace.

The love and grace of God serve as the foundation for all that we as Brethren in Christ hold dear. It is divine love and grace that forgives the unforgivable, and it is that same love and grace that provides generously for the broken and needy. Literally everything else that we value begins and ends here: God offers each one of us the free gift of salvation in Christ Jesus, and he transforms us through the power of the Holy Spirit.

The God We Experience

Because the Brethren in Christ were born in a revival movement that emphasized genuine Christian conversion, experiencing God has always been a part of our church's identity. We value each person's story of how Jesus found them and brought new meaning to their lives. We believe everyone needs to acknowledge the living Christ, believe his promises, accept his call to follow him, and receive his transforming power. Salvation is a Person to person encounter!

In this encounter, however, the Bible specifically portrays God as the one who actively engages us in the drama of salvation. This is the theme that runs through Scripture from Genesis to Revelation. Again and again, God lovingly and graciously reaches out to ordinary human beings.

Numerous biblical passages illustrate this theme, but Exodus 3:1-15 and John 20:19-31 stand out as two prime examples. In Exodus 3, God revealed himself to Moses by means of a bush that, though blazing with fire, was not destroyed. In so doing, God disclosed his intention to redeem his people from slavery in Egypt. Moses inquired after the name of the God who was calling him to this task. He expected a noun, since nouns by definition designate people and things. Instead, God answered, "I AM WHO I AM" (vs. 14). While it is difficult to capture the full force of this word, God's response clearly illustrates that he is best known by his actions. Rather than experiencing God in some sort of mystical or theoretical vacuum, we come to know God through his works in human history and by his activity in our lives.

In John 20, Jesus met most of his disciples on the evening of the first Easter day. They were in hiding, but he knew where to find them. Suddenly, he entered their concealed room without picking the lock on the door! He then breathed his Spirit into the lives of these confused and fearful followers, and he gave them the task of delivering people who were enslaved to sin. The disciples who had themselves experienced Jesus' transforming presence in their lives were now sent to offer that same transforming grace to others.

Together these stories reveal a great deal about the God we experience. Among other things, he is both active and personal.

God is Active

The opening verse of the book of Genesis simply reads, "In the beginning when God created the heavens and the earth." This is not the typical way that books about God begin. But the God of Scripture surprises us. He chooses to introduce himself to us, and he makes his character known by the actions he performs. That is why Scripture contains so many narratives or stories describing God's many and varied activities. Long before someone coined the expression, "actions speak louder than words," God chose his deeds to reveal his person and his purposes.

God's creation and his involvement in history, therefore, are the loudspeakers through which we begin to learn of his nature and power (Rom. 1:20). His call to Abraham (Gen. 12) established the truth of one God in a world that believed in many gods. His redemptive love appeared in the call of Moses to deliver Israel from Egypt (Exod. 3), and the law given at Sinai trumpeted God's holiness and the expectations that he has for his people (Exod. 20). As Israel entered Canaan, God's trustworthiness was confirmed, for he had kept the promise of land that he swore earlier to Abraham (Josh. 1-12; cf. Gen. 12:1). Later, when he removed Israel from that same land because of their sins, God demonstrated his justice and sovereignty (2 Kings 25). Finally, when God protected his punished people and brought them back home, he forever revealed himself as a God of love and mercy (Ezra 1-2). Unmistakably, God rules over all things, including the ongoing affairs of individuals and nations.

But the clearest window into God's heart is the drama of salvation played out in the Old and New Testaments. In the Old Testament, he chose a nation to be his witnesses, gave them his Word, and established a family line through whom the Savior would come into the world. In the New Testament, the story reaches its climax. The Messiah is born, ministers in God's name, is crucified, and then resurrected with power and glory. All of this grows out of the simple fact that God wills to save people from the sin which destroys them (John 3:16).

From the creation of the world to the glory of heaven, God is the primary actor in the universe. He takes center stage and announces his presence. He is not resting offstage while the cast of human characters wear themselves out in a frantic search to find him, nor is he listening in the wings until some person finally figures out the mystery of God or develops the perfect doctrinal formula. Rather, God is the leading character in redemption, and his role gives meaning to the drama.

God is Relational

The purpose of Scripture is to make God known to us. But the word "know" can mean different things. It can refer to possessing basic information, as when I am aware of an upcoming appointment or recall someone's name. Beyond this, the word "know" can also indicate a deeper experience with something. Especially when we speak of knowing a person, the word signifies an intimate relationship that goes beyond possessing simple information. To know is to experience.

The Scripture contains extensive information. Reciting such information, however, is not what the Bible means by "knowing God." Salvation is not an award given to people who can pass a stiff test on the Bible. Many in Jesus' day could surely have done so, but they still missed the Messiah. Instead, Jesus blesses those who come to know him by a chosen relationship of trust and obedience. Their experience with Christ gives meaning and perspective to everything else in life. This is the true knowledge of God which Scripture intends for all of us to enjoy.

This intimate knowledge of God is also the only thing that will satisfy our human nature. We don't just collect bread recipes; we want to eat bread. Reading books on marriage is not our goal; we want to be married. Members of a sports team want to win the championship game, not simply read about another team's success. In the same way, we do not just want to read a theological description about God; we want to experience God in our lives.

The God who met Moses at the bush and who encountered the disciples in the upper room was a God who invited them to be in relationship with him. In the Old Testament God sometimes called Israel his wife (Hos. 2), or referred to the Hebrew people as his son (Exod. 4:22). Later, Jesus called his disciples his "friends" (John 15:14). Terms like these underscore intimate relationships between people and God.

Before his encounter with the burning bush, Moses knew about the "God of our Fathers," yet he asked to know God's name. Moses needed a personal relationship with God to accomplish the task assigned to him. In the New Testament, Thomas missed Jesus' first visit to the upper room. It took a personal meeting with Jesus to convince Thomas that Jesus was alive again (John 20:24-29). It is helpful to know "the God of our fathers" and to hear the testimony of those who have "seen Jesus." But a personal relationship with God is the only way to satisfy the biblical standard of the knowledge of God.

The God Who Saves

To know God, to enter into a Person-to-person relationship with him and to become a member of his family, is what the Bible means by salvation. Our spiritual sense tells us this is what we need. But often another voice tries to talk us out of the relationship with God that we long to have. "Maybe this is something that only a few privileged people can experience. Maybe God only wants a few chosen friends at his party and not a houseful of assorted people. Maybe you must belong to the right ethnic group, be born with special moral aptitudes, or have a psyche which is prone to 'spiritual experiences.' Possibly such a relationship with God is too costly, like those desirable things you see while shopping which are beyond your budget. There is not enough cash in your character bank to purchase friendship with God."

Many people settle for window shopping for God's salvation. They would not think of going into the store and making a fool of themselves. For as soon as they ask for the product on display, the clerk will want to know how they will pay for it. If only they had the courage to risk the asking! Alarmingly, the price tag reads: "Free to all who ask for it. Paid in full by the lavish love of God, spent to the last penny when Christ died for sinners on a Roman cross in Jerusalem." Yet that is precisely what Ephesians 2:8-10 declares:

> For by grace you have been saved through faith, and this is not your own doing; it is the gift of God—not the result of works, so that no one may boast. For we are what he has made us, created in Christ Jesus for good works, which God prepared beforehand to be our way of life.

Although we are sinners and undeserving of his favor, God loves us. Although we cannot earn salvation by our own good efforts, God frees us. And although we are sick and weak, God heals us. Rather than being an unpleasable tyrant, God is a parent who gives freely to his children the gifts of love that they need. Believing in Jesus and accepting the power of his death and resurrection opens for us the very doors of heaven.

But free gifts might very well have certain conditions attached. Just as we would not give a priceless heirloom to someone who does not want it and refuses to care for it, so God does not save those who refuse his mercy and have no intention of recognizing his authority over the conduct of their lives. That is why the Bible requires repentance and faith of those who would be saved (Acts 2:38; 16:31). Repentance involves genuine sorrow for past sins and a sincere intention to live differently in the future. In the same way that we cannot have a meaningful relationship with people if we constantly do things that offend them, so we cannot experience intimacy with God unless we are willing to live as he wants us to (Matt. 16:24).

To speak rightly of salvation as a gift, we must further comprehend the nature of the gift we are considering. We can give material gifts to people which, from that point on, become their personal property to do with as they please. Or we can give gifts that are real, though intangible. For example, we can give someone time, care, love, or respect. These latter gifts are relational rather than material. They do not become the personal property of the recipient and cannot be enjoyed unless one stays in relationship with the giver. Salvation is a gift of the second kind and not of the material kind. It is a relationship with God that confers great benefits, like a child's relationship with her parents or a man's relationship with his wife. It is not a thing that we can say we own as a property right. It is a relationship that must be maintained if we are to experience its benefit.

Closely related to this is the way we talk about experiencing salvation. We often think of experiences as events that have a calendar date associated with them. We have birthdays, graduations, wedding anniversaries, and photographs of other memorable incidents of our lives. In one sense those are unrepeatable events, things that can never be experienced again in exactly the same way. Salvation is like that in one respect. Many of us can remember our spiritual birthday, when we decided to live no more without God and entered into a life of peace. Salvation had a point of beginning that we can date. But since salvation is a relationship with God, we continue to experience it every day of our Christian life.

Marriage is perhaps a good illustration of the point. Marriage is consummated on a particular day. But when we talk about the experience of marriage, we mean more than what occurred in a particular twenty-four-hour period. We mean what began on that day and everything that developed since then. Salvation, like marriage, is both an event and a process. At some point in time, we respond to God's loving and gracious invitation, and he saves us from our sins. In that moment, our relationship to God is consummated and we *begin* a new life in Christ Jesus. That moment, however, is only the beginning.

The God Who Transforms

It would have been interesting to sit in Moses' tent the evening of his "burning bush" experience. How soon did the family know that something unusual had happened during his work day? How did he explain meeting God and being assigned a task? Such events leave a mark on a person! Before long the whole family was involved in his career change. They went with him to Egypt, the place Moses had avoided for forty years because it held memories of the worst failure of his life (Exod. 2). Moses' earlier attempt to deliver Israel from slavery resulted in his committing murder, and he was distrusted by Israel and hated by Pharaoh because of it.

Now, Moses went back to Egypt a changed man. Not only had he matured and mellowed, he had met God in a life-transforming way. Moses had seen the Lord, and that vision changed the way he saw himself and others. Times of frustration, perplexity, and even failure occasionally recurred (i.e., Num. 20), but the course of his life reflects a permanent change in his character. Moses succeeded because God had made him a "new man."

The story of the disciples in John 20 is similar. Jesus met them, quite likely in the same upper room where they had eaten the Last Supper. It was the place that reminded them of both the failure of their faith and of their courage. Jesus' appearance to them as resurrected Lord restored both their faith and their career. They now knew that God's plan to redeem humanity had not suffered defeat when Jesus was crucified on Good Friday. Far from it. In less than three days' time, Satan was defeated, sin destroyed, and death conquered! Jesus not only rewound the clock of human history, he changed its direction as well. No longer would the creeping darkness of evil threaten to snuff out the flickering candle of God's truth. Indeed, the light that flashed from Christ's grave will continue to shine until even the remotest places on earth see the truth of God.

A lot happened to the disciples in that upper room. First, they were restored in their relationship with Christ, Peter leading the way in confession (John 21) as he earlier had led the way in declaring that Jesus was the Messiah (Mark 8). Jesus then gave them a grand tour through the Old Testament that made clear God's intention to redeem all people by means of Christ's death and resurrection (Luke 24:25-49). Thirdly, he gave them the task of spreading the benefits of salvation throughout the world. And finally, Jesus breathed upon them the Holy Spirit, who would energize them for the work that awaited them. Like the medicines we take in capsule form, with timed release benefits to our body, this breath of Jesus became the wind of Pentecost fifty days later in this same room (Acts 2). Filled with the Spirit's power, these disciples found their voices for praise and for preaching. Their encounter with Jesus had radically transformed them!

The testimony of all God's people through the ages is that coming to know God in a real relationship is a transforming event (2 Cor. 5:17). When I think of this truth, I am reminded of those special artists who have the ability to restore old paintings. Many old churches, for example, have covered over ancient art with layers of plaster or superimposed paint. But art restorers can get down through the covering layers to the original work, and touch it up with fresh paint until the luster of the original appears.

Although humans were created in the "image of God" (Gen. 1:27), sin has all but hidden this original portrait. God, however, is the world's foremost expert in art reclamation. Christ dissolves the layers of corruption; his blood wipes away the disgraceful pictures of our lives. And what appears is the renewed image of God in us (Rom. 8:29; 2 Cor. 3:18; Col. 3:10). For the God who breathes the life of his Spirit into us today is the Creator who breathed his likeness into humans at the beginning of history (Gen. 2:7). God is a transforming agent: mud becomes a person; sinners become saints; cowards become people of courageous conviction; the mute burst forth with praise; and the indolent find a mission that launches them into a life of active service for the kingdom of God. With love and grace, the God who saves us continues to transform us, restoring in us the beauty of himself.

Conclusion

I was almost ten years old when I decided to respond to the voice of God, a voice which I first heard nearly two years earlier. Even in the simplicity of those childhood years, two things had kept me from making a Christian commitment. I did not want to admit that I was a sinner, and I had no interest in acknowledging Jesus publicly as my Savior and Lord.

On this particular night, I lay awake in bed long after everyone else in the house had fallen asleep. Like the young girl lost in the mountains of central Pennsylvania, I felt far from God and frighteningly alone. Finally, I threw back the covers, got out of bed, and made my way to my parents' bedroom. When they asked me what was wrong, I told them I needed to be saved and wanted them to pray with me. The three of us knelt by their bed, while I confessed my sin and my need for Christ to be my Savior. In the morning we shared my decision with my four older sisters, and, before the summer was over, I publicly confessed my faith in Jesus through baptism and church membership. Unmistakably, God met me at the level of my childhood understanding.

In the fifty years since that night, I have come to understand and to experience God's love and grace in far deeper and richer measures. Many of the years of early adulthood were consumed with unrealistic notions of what it takes to please God. In recent years I have been relieved to discover that my salvation depends much more upon God's active love for me than upon my efforts for him. Further, the earlier passion for information about God has slowly given way to a more balanced and intimate relationship with God himself. Although often at a pace and by means that I did not anticipate, the God who saves me continues to transform every area of my life. As the apostle Paul expressed it, I am being transformed "from one degree of glory to another" (2 Cor. 3:18).

My story is not an exact duplicate of Moses' story or that of the disciples of Jesus, and neither will yours be. The important thing for all of us is that we genuinely experience the same God that they encountered. When we receive the free gift of salvation and are transformed by the power of the Holy Spirit, our lives become contemporary testimonies to God's wonderful love and grace. Settling for secondhand information simply will not do.

Discussion Questions

1. Why do the Brethren in Christ emphasize conversion?

2. Since God takes an active role in our salvation, is there anything we need to do to experience it?

   Rep-/Believe

3. What does it mean "to know" God? How might your understanding of the word affect the way you live out the Christian faith.

   Relational

4. Is it possible to be a Christian but not know it? Or to be a Christian without others recognizing it?

5. Dietrich Bonhoeffer spoke of "costly grace." If salvation is a free gift, where is the "cost" in grace?

   > obedience

6. Share a time in your life when grace became vivid for you. What lasting effects might this experience have brought?

7. The Bible speaks so much about God's love. Why do you think we have so much difficulty believing it in our lives? Can you think of any particular hindrances to affirming God's love in your own life?

8. How has knowing God transformed your life? Are you aware of ways in which that transforming process continues in your life today?

9. Which of the following two statements best describes your Christian experience? (1) "Following Jesus has produced a

growing appreciation of God's love and grace in my life"; or (2) "Grace seemed amazing when I was converted, but the task of being a Christian leaves me feeling like I'm not worthy enough for God to be pleased with me."

10. How can you know that you have a real and intimate relationship with God? What assurances do you have?

Cultivate relationship - Obedience
- Allow the Spirit to guide

For Further Reading

Jones, E. Stanley. *Conversion*. Nashville, Tenn.: Abingdon Press, 1959.

Lewis, C. S. *Surprised by Joy*. New York: Harcourt, Brace and World, 1955.

Simons, Menno. "Confession and the New Birth." No. 5 in the series of Mennonite Sources and Documents. Translated and edited by Irvin B. Horst. Lancaster, Pa.: Lancaster Mennonite Historical Society, 1996.

Smith, Timothy L. *Whitfield and Wesley on the New Birth*. Grand Rapids, Mich.: Zondervan Publishing House (Francis Asbury Press), 1986.

Wingert, Norman A. *Twice Born: A Book of Conversion Stories*. Grand Rapids, Mich.: Zondervan Publishing House, 1955.

2

Believing the Bible

*We value the Bible as God's authoritative Word,
study it together, and build our lives on its truth.*

by John R. Yeatts

*All Scripture is inspired by God and is useful for
teaching, for reproof, for correction, and for training in
righteousness, so that everyone who belongs to God
may be proficient, equipped for every good work.*
—The Apostle Paul (2 Timothy 3:16-17)

Last evening, while shopping in the King of Prussia Mall outside of Philadelphia, I wandered into a bookstore and found myself browsing through the "Bible" section. I was amazed at the variety of Bibles I encountered there. Being an inveterate researcher, I asked my wife for a pencil and paper and wrote a sampling of the Bibles I saw on the shelf. In addition to the typical translations and paraphrases (King James Version, New King James Version, Revised Standard Version, New Revised Standard Version, New International Version, The Living Bible, The Message, etc.) was a remarkable array of study and devotional Bibles: God's Little Devotional Bible for Women, the Women's Study Bible, the Student Bible, the Teen Study Bible, the Student's Life Application Bible, the Spirit Filled Life Application Bible for Students, the Youth Walk

Devotional Bible, the Spiritual Formation Bible, the Inspirational Bible, the NIV Children's Bible, the Couples' Devotional Bible, the Collegiate Devotional Bible, the Original African American Study Bible, the One Year Bible, and the Catholic Bible. *The Other Bible,* which includes books not found in the official canon of the church, and *The Complete Book of Bible Trivia* also appeared. Surprisingly, I found all of these Bibles, not in a Christian Light Bookstore, but in Walden Books! In an age trumpeted as secular, the Bible remains astoundingly popular.

Indeed, the Bible continues to be the focus for Christian reading. I remember my wife teaching a survey of the Old Testament to an adult Sunday school class. She challenged the class to read the Old Testament through. A number of class members took up the challenge and even carried their Bibles with them to work. Apparently, these class members are not unique. According to Search Institute's *A National Study of Protestant Congregations,* 77 percent of adults say they are "interested" or "very interested" in studying the Bible.[1] As Sara P. Little, Professor of Christian Education at Union Seminary in Virginia, explains:

> There is a genuine longing for some frame of reference and authority, some common history and language, some source of meaning, all of which point to a kind of expectancy people have when they think of the Bible.[2]

Even young Christians at times demonstrate the same excitement about reading the Bible. Some years ago, my son came to my wife and handed over his favorite video game so that he would have more time to study for Bible quizzing.

Moreover, the Bible continues to fascinate non-Christians. During the last two years, I taught a class at Temple University, an institution which started out as a Baptist school for ministerial training but has become a secular university. In that setting, I taught sections of a general education course required of all of Temple's more than 20,000 undergraduates. The course has a unit on religion in which students read portions of Genesis and Exodus and the entire Gospel of Matthew. One of my students was a postal worker. He told me that this was the first time he had read the Bible and that he was enjoying the required reading for the course. He even took the Bible to work to read at lunch. A Jewish student came to me and said that she had a friend who was interested in reading the Bible and asked: "Where should she start?" When told that the friend was also Jewish, I suggested that she begin with the book of Genesis.

Documenting this remarkable interest in the Bible, a Gallup Poll taken at the beginning of this decade reported that nearly every household in North America has a Bible and stated, "By now so many Bibles have been printed in this country, and continue to be printed by the millions each year, that even rough estimates of the total number published to date do not exist."[3] Certainly, the Bible has been and remains a compelling book for Jews, Christians, and even secularists. What is the reason for this popularity? The Brethren in Christ, among other Christians, believe it is because the Bible is the authoritative Word of God.

God's Authoritative Word

At the most fundamental level Christians believe that Jesus Christ, God's Son, is the "Word made flesh." Although the phrase, "Word of God," primarily refers in the Bible to Christ himself (John 1), Christians believe that both the Old and New Testaments are the authoritative and reliable written Word of God. Some Christians use words like inerrancy and infallibility to describe the authority of the Bible. These words themselves have become divisive and are not found anywhere in Scripture. We prefer to speak of the Bible using its own words—revelation, authority, and inspiration.

Revelation

My wife and I enjoy watching mysteries on Public Television. Our favorite detective is Agatha Christie's character Hercule Poirot. We like trying to figure out who committed the murder and await with great anticipation the end of the program when Inspector Poirot identifies the culprit and explains how he solved the mystery. Can you imagine our reaction if, at the end of a program, we were told that the identity of the guilty person remained unknown? We would feel cheated for watching an entire show without being rewarded with the insight that we were waiting for. A mystery is not something unknown but something that is revealed to a special group. In the case of PBS mysteries, Hercule Poirot reveals the identity of the guilty person to those who watch the movie. In the case of the Bible, the mystery of God's salvation through Christ is revealed to those who read prayerfully and expectantly.

The word "reveal" means to uncover, disclose, or bring to light, and it frequently appears in the Bible with reference to the divine revelation of supernatural mysteries.[4] In the Old Testament, for example, God revealed himself to Moses and Aaron during the Exodus (Exod. 5:1-3), and the "secret things" of God were revealed to the Israelites who obeyed the Law (Deut. 29:29; cf. 1 Sam. 2:27). Later, the word of the Lord was also revealed to Samuel (2 Sam. 3:21) and the prophets (Isa. 22:14). In the New Testament, Jesus says that divine knowledge has been handed over to him; knowledge which he will reveal to whomever he chooses (Matt. 11:25-27; Luke 10:21-22). Likewise, Jesus' messiahship, eternal life and the love of God, the mystery of Christ, and the wisdom and righteousness of God have also been revealed.[5] Finally, Jesus himself indicates that when the kingdom comes the Son of Man will be revealed (Luke 17:30; cf. Col. 3:4; 2 Thess. 1:7-8; 1 Pet. 5:1; 1 John 2:28). Clearly, revelation is a theme repeated throughout the biblical record.

Revelation focuses on the most basic question about God's communication with humanity: Has God spoken? Persons who believe the atheistic versions of such modern systems as Marxism, humanism, and existentialism all answer this question, "No. God has not spoken." Nevertheless, all Christians join the other world religions by affirming that God has indeed spoken. Specifically, Christians believe that God has communicated truth about Jesus Christ coming into the world to bring salvation to those who believe in him and commit themselves to obeying him. Although the Bible was composed by human agents, preserved by human copiers, and canonized by church councils, the Bible ultimately has its origin in God and has been preserved in transmission by the Holy Spirit. It is precisely because the Bible is ultimately the result of God's revelation that it is seen as carrying such unique authority.

Authority

Today, authority is not a popular word. In a postmodern age, investing total authority in any one source is seen as imperialistic and oppressive. This week, I went to see *Dogma*, a movie about two fallen angels who devised a plan to trick God and gain entrance to heaven. Most of my Christian friends were scandalized by the offensive language of the angels and even the apostles. While this bothered me, I was more troubled by the philosophy that the movie communicated. The basic message was that the important thing is not what you believe, but that your "heart is in the right place." While it may be true that dogma has at times been made too important among Christians, the rejection of divine authority for personal subjective truth is at odds with the Bible.

We live in an age of individualism and self-actualization. People tend to look within themselves for truth. Yet, Christians believe that the only way to God is through Christ, and that the Bible is the only source of knowledge about Christ. Jesus said to Thomas, "I am the way, and the truth, and the life. No one comes to the Father except through me" (John 14:6). This belief in the sole authority of Christ and his revelation in the Scriptures is a scandal in today's world, but it is the scandal that Christians are forced to live with if they are to be faithful to the Bible.

The word "authority" denotes ability, right, or power. The concept of authority means that the Bible has a divine basis.[6] The word occurs quite often in the Bible. At the end of the Sermon on the Mount, the astonished crowds said that Jesus "taught as one having authority" (Matt. 7:29; cf. Mark 1:21-28; Luke 4:31-37). His authority is further recognized when he heals the paralytic after forgiving his sins (Matt. 9:6-8; Mark 2:5-12; Luke 5:17-26). This authority is then passed on by Jesus to his disciples (Matt. 10:1;

Mark 3:14-15; 6:7; Luke 9:1; cf. Matt. 21:23-27; Mark 11:27-33; Luke 20:1-9). At the end of his ministry, before he left this world, Jesus told his disciples that "All authority in heaven and on earth has been given to me" (Matt. 28:18). John's gospel affirms that the Son of Man is given "authority to execute judgment" (5:27) and to give eternal life (17:3). Paul implies that his own words are based on divine authority (1 Cor. 9:8; 1 Thess. 4:8) and even recognizes that at times he speaks without this authority (2 Cor. 11:17). The author of the Pastoral Epistles says that authority is passed on to Titus (Titus 2:15). Although authority is not specifically attributed to the Bible itself, as the written record of God, it can be seen in a derivative sense to carry the authority given by God to Christ.

Some Christians who grant the priority of the Bible also insist that other sources of authority stand alongside the Bible. Roman Catholics, for example, have historically affirmed that church tradition is an authority parallel to the Bible. Likewise, liberation theologians, who witness to the authority of the Bible and often interpret the Scriptures quite literally, typically start with an analysis of the historical situation of oppression before they turn to biblical reflection. Nevertheless, many Christians, including the Brethren in Christ, continue to affirm the Reformation doctrine of *sola scriptura*, the sole authority of the Scriptures. Although these Christians agree with the wider church that people can learn something about God through nature and reason, they maintain that believers have received a special revelation of God in the person of Christ and the record of Christ's incarnation in the Holy Scriptures. Thus, the Bible is the final source of authority. The reason is that the Scriptures are the inspired written record of (1) the prophets who anticipated the coming of Christ, (2) the Gospels that record the words and deeds of Christ the Word, and (3) the Acts, epistles, and Revelation which proclaim the teaching of Christ for the church. Hence, in a real sense, the Bible is the inspired written Word of God.

Inspiration

When my children were little and I was working for the church, I remember saying to them, "This week, I'd like to take you on a picnic" (or some other outing that they enjoyed). Usually, I followed through on my intentions. Yet, as all parents will attest, there were times when I had to change the plans. At those times, I can remember my children saying, "You promised." I would respond, "I did not promise. I simply said that I'd like to take you, but something has come up that I cannot control." For me to cancel such a family outing took a major emergency. Yet, at times it did happen.

We sometimes treat God's written word like my young children treated my comments to them. Because God said certain words, we assume that he meant what we think he meant. Although it is difficult for little children to determine what their parents mean by the words they use, we have the obligation to find out what God intended by the words of the Bible. We should not insert our theology or modern interpretations of science and history into the text of Scripture.

That the Bible is inspired literally means it is "God-breathed." Although the word is rarely used in the Bible, the importance given to 2 Timothy 3:16 in talking about the authority of the Bible makes it a key concept. The passage claims, "All Scripture is inspired by God." Elsewhere, Paul notes that the Thessalonians "received the word with joy inspired by the Holy Spirit" (1 Thess. 1:6).

Many evangelical groups have spent much time arguing about theories of inspiration. As was mentioned before, two basic theories of inspiration have been common in the evangelical world— inerrancy and infallibility. Inerrancy claims that the Bible is without error in all that it literally says. The Bible makes no mistakes regarding theology and faith, but it is also without error in matters of science, history, psychology, sociology, and everything else. The Scriptures carry the final word when the general revelation of nature and reason seems to conflict with special revelation of Christ and the Bible. The second position tries to be more open to natural revelation. It holds that the Bible is infallible in areas that it intended to teach–religion, theology, faith, morality–but may not be without error in areas where God primarily speaks through general revelation–science, history, sociology, psychology. For example, the biblical account of creation teaches theological truths about God creating the world, not the time it took to create the world. The genealogies are constructed for theological reasons rather than as a source for learning historical chronologies. The subordination of women to men may describe the first century culture but not be God's standard.

It is sometimes difficult to determine what God is intending to communicate through his word. There is great danger in rejecting biblical ideas simply because they do not fit with our ideas about theology, science, or psychology. Yet, we cannot impose our meaning on God's words like my children translated my intentions to spend the day with them into an unbreakable promise to do so. The most important issue is indeed that God has spoken through the Bible. It is the responsibility of the reader of Scripture to determine what God intends to say and not demand that the Bible say more than that.

Study the Bible Together

As was stated earlier, the average North American household has at least one copy of the Bible. Yet, people are remarkably illiterate regarding the content of the Bible. In 1990, only half of the adults surveyed in a Gallup Poll could name any of the four Gospels, and just 37 percent could name all four. In a 1982 survey, only 42 percent of adults were able to correctly identify as many as five of the ten commandments and only 42 percent could identify Jesus as the person who delivered the Sermon on the Mount.[7] This situation has led pollster George Gallup to conclude that "Americans revere the Bible—but, by and large, they don't read it. And because they don't read it, they have become a nation of biblical illiterates."[8]

According to 2 Timothy 3:16-17, once again, the reason that the

Bible is inspired by God is that it "is useful for teaching, for reproof, for correction, and for training in righteousness, so that everyone who belongs to God may be proficient, equipped for every good work." If a primary characteristic of the Bible is its usefulness, it must be read and applied in the life of the church and in the lives of Christians as they interact in the world. A crucial question then becomes, how is the Bible to be interpreted so that it can be applicable to life?

Just Read the Bible and Do What it Says

Some Christians claim to be literalists. Their approach to the Bible is simple: "Read it and do what it says." Yet, it must be recognized that such a principle is naive; the Bible requires interpretation. To fail to recognize this leads to persons imposing their own understandings of Scripture on others and rejecting persons who do not agree with them. Furthermore, such a principle of interpretation can turn into a "monkey see, monkey do" mentality. One could consult spiritual mediums based on the example of Saul, lust after other women and commit adultery emulating David, and brutalize enemies modeling the example of Solomon. Clearly, this approach is problematic. A better way to interpret the Bible is to see it through the life and teaching of Jesus Christ, our perfect example.

Christ at the Center

All Christians tend to emphasize some part of the Bible over others. The Brethren in Christ have typically thought it appropriate to start with Jesus Christ and to read the Old Testament in the light of its fulfillment in Christ and the epistles as the implementation of Christ's message. Indeed, the Bible itself recognizes a progressive revelation in which God spoke in the past through the prophets, but has given a final and complete revelation in Christ (Heb.1:1-2). Practically, this means that Christians should not selectively use the Old Testament to condone things for which Jesus brought a new standard. For example, Jesus' teachings about refraining from resisting evil should be given priority over the divine approval to go to war in the Old Testament. Moreover, Jesus' teaching regarding the monogamous relationship of husband and wife, which serves as a prototype of Christ and the church, should take precedence over the permission given for divorce and polygamous relationships in the Hebrew Scriptures.

Interpreted by the Gathered Church

Throughout history, the Roman Catholic Church saw itself as the interpreter of the Scriptures. Accordingly, Church officials interpreted the Bible for the people. The Protestant Reformation rejected this, making everyone a priest before God and an interpreter of the Word of God. The Anabaptists were uneasy with both of these extremes, holding that the church as the visible body of God's people has the responsibility to interpret the Bible for the community. Indeed, it seems that the Bible is best interpreted, not by the institutional church hierarchy, nor by the individual Christian. The former leads to legalism and the latter to relativism. Instead, Christians should interpret the Bible together, listening to the insights of others and being held accountable by fellow interpreters.

While all Christians, regardless of their training, are able to interpret the Bible responsibly, they should be informed by sound biblical scholarship. Two examples of the findings of biblical scholarship that are relevant to Christians' interpreting the Bible will have to suffice here. First, genre studies have pointed out that the Bible is a library of many books written over a period of hundreds of years utilizing a variety of literary types: narrative, law, poetry, drama, prophecy, gospel, letter, and apocalyptic. The assumption of this research is that the poetic language of the Bible is interpreted different from the narrative accounts. For instance, the poetic statement, "all the trees of the field shall clap their hands" (Isa. 55:12), gives a strange meaning when interpreted with a flat-footed literalism. More significantly, the refrain in Genesis 1, "there was evening and there was morning, the first (second, third, etc.) day," may be poetic rather than chronological detail. Job, which begins,

"There was once a man in the land of Uz whose name was Job" and continues with friends who arrive and speak to Job in extended poetic verse, may be drama rather than history. Jesus certainly uses fictitious parables and occasionally includes humor—the "log" and "speck" (Matt. 7:3-5)—and hyperbolic overstatement—"hate your father and mother" (Luke 14:26), "cut off your hands and pluck out your eyes" (Matt. 5:29-30). It is important for Christians to recognize the literary nature of the Scriptures. Christians must walk the careful line of taking the teachings of the Bible seriously and yet respecting the symbolic language that it contains.

Another result of biblical research is the investigation of the historical and cultural contexts of the Bible. The literalistic approach of "read the Bible and do what it says" has led some Christians among us to "greet one another with a kiss of love" (1 Pet. 5:14) and some Christian women to cover their heads because they should always be in an attitude of prayer (1 Cor. 11:5). Today, these practices and others have been given cultural explanations. In the case of the holy kiss, it is now thought that the practice of greeting with a kiss is no longer common and could even be misunderstood. Regarding the prayer covering, most Christians today call attention to the cultural setting of the New Testament when all respectable women covered their heads in normal social contacts. They suggest that perhaps Christian women in realizing their new freedom in Christ were abandoning a social custom and bringing themselves and the church of Christ into disrepute. Because culture today does not expect women to cover their heads, the situation Paul was addressing is no longer relevant.

There is, of course, the danger of throwing out the proverbial baby with the bath water. In the process of abandoning the literal practice of the holy kiss, we may also undermine the intimate fellowship that it symbolized, and in discarding the prayer covering also lose the respect for Christ as the head of the church. Again, Christians should diligently interpret scripture with the tools that biblical scholarship has provided, but be careful in the process to treat the text with respect and integrity.

Build Our Lives on Its Truth

In the process of studying together, we continually affirm that the Bible contains truth for Christians to build their lives around. Nevertheless, it does not seem that most persons view the Bible in this way. Five hundred telephone interviews and forty face-to-face conversations with baby boomers confirmed in the Presbyterian Church (U.S.A.) revealed that, although 52 percent are enrolled members and attend church at least six times a year, 75 percent had dropped out of the church at one time or another. The reason given by most subjects for this was not because of the church's positions on theological or moral issues, but because "religion itself had become low on their list of personal priorities."[9] The researchers indicate that the problem seems to be a lack of spiritual conviction. They charge the church with losing "the will and ability to teach the Christian faith."[10] What is particularly distressing is to see leaders in the Christian community who believe that the Bible is the inerrant or infallible word of God who do not follow what the Bible teaches and fall into the sins of adultery, greed, and power-seeking. The truth is that it does no good to proclaim the inspiration of Scripture unless the Bible is obeyed and used in the life of the church and individual Christians.

The story is told of a poor jeweler who was arrested and placed in prison for a crime that he did not commit.[11] After several months, the jeweler's wife came to the prison and told the guards that her husband was a devout man who prayed regularly and needed his prayer rug. The guards agreed that a prayer rug was harmless and allowed him this one possession. Like Daniel, the jeweler prayed several times a day for weeks. Finally, he said to the jailers:

> I am bored sitting here day after day with nothing to do. I am a good jeweler and if you will let me have some pieces of metal and some simple tools, I will make you jewelry. You could then sell what I make at the bazaar and add to your low salaries as jailers. I ask for little—just something to fill the idle hours and keep my skill in practice.[12]

The jailers agreed and brought the metal and tools. Each evening, they would take home the jewelry that was made that day along with the tools and excess metal. One morning months later, when the jailers came to the cell, the jeweler was gone with no evidence of how he had escaped.

Finally, the real criminal was arrested for the crime for which the jeweler was imprisoned. Subsequently, one of the jailers saw the jeweler in the market, and asked him how he had escaped. The jeweler explained that his wife had gone to the architect of the prison and obtained the blueprints of the cell doors and locks. She had these designed into the prayer rug she had made for her husband. As he prayed each day, the jeweler began to see the design in the rug. From the blueprint of the lock for his room, he made a key using the metal and tools provided for him. Thus, the prayer rug was the design for his liberation from prison.

Likewise, the Bible is our design for salvation and the new life in Christ. Yet, in the same way that the jeweler had the ability to interpret the rug, we must develop the skill for interpreting the Bible and applying it in our lives. In general there are two steps to applying the Bible. First, one must know what the Bible means, and, second, one must decide the Bible's significance for daily life.[13] A previous section noted that the Bible's meaning is best interpreted by the gathered community opening it together and reading through the lens of Christ. Finding the significance of the text for the life of the individual believer is a different matter. When the gathered church has done this in a rather rigid manner, legalism has resulted.

Instead, it seems that the significance of the text is determined by the believer under the influence of the Holy Spirit. Some churches have allowed the Holy Spirit full reign in determining the meaning of the Bible. This has resulted in a multitude of interpretations by persons all believing that they were guided by the Holy Spirit. While the gathered believers are important for understanding the Bible, considerable flexibility must be given the Holy Spirit to lead the believer in finding the personal significance of the text. By giving the community the task of interpreting the Bible, we avoid the subjectivism of some of our brothers and sisters who have relied on the Spirit for interpretation. On the other hand, consulting the Holy Spirit in applying the Bible to our lives allows us to avoid the legalism of many of our brothers and sisters who have applied the decisions of the gathered community in a rigid and legalistic manner.

More specifically, when we decide what clothing to wear, the biblical principle of modesty applied under the leadership of the Holy Spirit helps the person to decide how that principle applies to their dress. The biblical principle of separation from the world is applied under the leadership of the Holy Spirit to help the Christian to determine what vocational and leisure activities are appropriate within the boundaries of biblical teaching. Thus the two principles complement each other in our understanding and application of the Bible. The communal interpretation of the Bible helps us to discern what the text is saying and the emphasis on the Holy Spirit's guidance helps us to find the significance of the text for our lives. The dynamic interaction between the Spirit and studious discernment is thereby maintained.

Some years ago, when my family moved for a year to Nairobi, Kenya, we experienced people begging for money every time we went downtown. Initially, I was compelled to give them some coins, but soon I became oblivious to their appeal. Yet, my daughter felt badly about passing the children without giving them anything. So she saved her coins, and when we went to town, she passed them out to the children begging. Although my daughter's actions were motivated by sympathy, she was certainly living out the words of Jesus: "Give to everyone who begs from you" (Matt. 5:42). She was practicing the truth of Scripture in her life.

Conclusion

"Believing the Bible" involves taking seriously both major parts of 2 Timothy 3:16-17. On the one hand, the Bible is the inspired word revealed by God and therefore fully authoritative for Christians. On the other hand, the Bible is useful to build our lives upon. This wholistic approach to the Bible will set us apart from many other Christians. On the one extreme, our fundamentalist brothers and sisters have often made their belief that the Bible is without error to be more important than the obligation to put it into practice in life. On the other extreme, liberal Christians have often played down the inspiration of the Bible and thus undercut the very basis needed for motivating people to be active in the social programs that are rightfully important to them. It is crucial to emphasize both the nature of the Bible as the authoritative and inspired revelation of God and the usefulness of the Bible for study and application to life. This is captured well in our second core value: "We value the Bible as God's authoritative Word, study it together, and build our lives on its truth."

Discussion Questions

1. What does 2 Timothy 3:16-17 teach us about the nature of the Bible and how we are to understand and apply it?

2. What does it mean that Jesus Christ is the Word of God? In what sense is the Bible the written Word? How are the two related and prioritized?

3. What are the meanings of the words revelation, authority and inspiration? Why does the author resist using the popular words like inerrancy and infallibility? Do you agree with this resistance?

4. Is the Bible the only revelation of God? What are the roles of reason, tradition, and experience in communicating or confirming God's revelation?

5. What does it mean that the Bible is inspired (God-breathed)? Is the Bible without error in areas of faith, history, science, chronology, etc.? Did the Bible intend to teach in these areas?

6. Is there anything wrong with just reading the Bible and doing what it says? Why might we need a more complex interpretative procedure?

7. Why does the author emphasize reading the Bible with Christ at the center? What have been some of the results of this emphasis?

8. Who is responsible for interpreting the Bible? The denomination? The local congregation? The individual? Why?

9. Is it important to consider the types of literature found in the Bible or the cultural setting in which the Bible was written? Do these not just allow persons to interpret the Bible as they please?

10. Do you believe that the Holy Spirit should be central in interpreting the meaning of the Bible or in determining how the Bible should be applied or both?

For Further Reading

Achtemeier, Paul J. *Authority and Inspiration: Nature and Function of Christian Scripture.* Revised and expanded ed. Peabody, Mass.: Hendrickson Publishers, 1999.

Fee, Gordon D. and Douglas Stuart. *How to Read the Bible for All It's Worth.* 2nd ed. Grand Rapids, Mich.: Zondervan Publishing House, 1993.

Stott, John R.W. *Understanding the Bible.* Expanded ed. Grand Rapids, Mich.: Zondervan Publishing House, 1999.

Thompson, David L. *Bible Study that Works.* Revised ed. Nappanee, Ind.: Evangel Publishing House, 1994.

Yoder, Perry B. *Toward Understanding the Bible: Hermeneutics for Lay People.* Newton, Kan.: Faith and Life Press, 1978.

3

Worshiping God

*We value heartfelt worship that is God-honoring,
Spirit-directed, and life-changing.*

by David L. Hall and Dwight W. Thomas

> *You awake us to delight in Your praise;*
> *for You made us for Yourself,*
> *and our hearts are restless until they rest in You.*
> *—St. Augustine (**Confessions**, Book One)*

Human beings were created to worship. Whether it be a child looking in awe at a sports figure, a teenager idolizing a popular musician, or an aspiring executive stopping at nothing to reach the top, all of us express a fundamental aspect of our humanity when we focus our passion on someone or something. In so doing, we worship (attribute "worth" to) whatever or whoever is the focus of our passion.

From the beginning, God intended that he be the object of our deepest affections. God's intentions, however, were ignored when Adam and Eve let the quest for personal knowledge, even the hope of being "like God," become their focus (Gen. 3:1-7). Since that time, human beings have put virtually everyone and everything imaginable ahead of God. This no doubt helps explain why the Bible repeatedly pleads:

> I am the Lord your God... you shall have no other gods before me. You shall not make for yourself an idol... (Exod. 20:2-4).

> No one can serve two masters; for a slave will either hate the one and love the other, or be devoted to the one and despise the other. You cannot serve God and wealth (Matt. 6:24).

> Put to death, therefore, whatever belongs to your earthly nature: sexual immorality, impurity, lust, evil desires and greed, which is idolatry (Col. 3:5; NIV).

Unmistakably, to center our devotion on anyone or anything other than God is sin.

With this in mind, we in the Brethren in Christ Church value heartfelt worship that is God-honoring, Spirit-directed, and life-changing. Worshiping the Lord, after all, is our highest calling and primary reason to be. As the writers of the Shorter Catechism so wonderfully captured this same idea nearly 400 years ago, "Man's chief end is to glorify God, and to enjoy him forever."[1]

The Meaning of Worship

If worshiping God occupies so central a role in the Christian life, then we must explore more fully what the term "worship" means. In the Old Testament, four different Hebrew words are translated into English as "worship." Of these, the most common denotes the act of "bowing down"or "doing homage" (i.e., Exod. 32:8; Deut. 29:26; Ps. 45:11). In the New Testament, the key Greek word for worship literally means "to kiss toward," and it conveys this same idea of showing reverence or doing obeisance (i.e., Matt. 2:11; Mark 5:6; Acts 10:25). A second important Greek word means "to serve"or "to minister," and a third gives us our English word, liturgy. By putting all of these ideas together, we see that worship involves attitudes (awe, reverence, respect) and actions (bowing, praising, serving).

Worship, therefore, is both an objective activity (we focus on the object of our worship) and a subjective experience (we ourselves are affected by our worship).

But how do we relate this to the way we actually worship God? To go back to an earlier observation, worship is both an attitude and an act. Because worship is so basic to human desire, we are foundationally affected by it. We feel that which thrills our hearts. This has been a positive emphasis of spiritual life in the Brethren in Christ Church, and our core value rightly affirms that genuine worship must be heartfelt. Worshiping God involves more than going through a series of religious motions or procedures. At the same time, however, genuine worship also involves more than experiencing a particular repertoire of feelings. As such, we must beware of the tendency to do whatever "feels right," a tendency fueled by our individualistic and relativistic culture. Given this need for balance and the importance of worship to the Christian life—and to the purposes and glory of God—it is imperative that an understanding of worship starts with God and not with ourselves.

God-honoring

In order to shift the focus of our worship to its rightful place, the first explicit emphasis in our core value is God-honoring. True worship begins with a right attitude toward God. Just to tie this issue of worship to the larger context of Christian truth, we cannot know to worship God—because of the effect of sin—unless God takes the first step. He has done that, and the invitation is for us, through his grace, to worship him. First of all, that means acknowledging that God is God. The way we do that is to admit, conversely, that we ourselves are insufficient for all our desires. It is an attitude of humility about ourselves and an attitude of awe and reverence toward God. In the words of the psalmist,

> When I look at your heavens, the work of your fingers...
> what are human beings that you are mindful of them,
> mortals that you care for them?
>
> O LORD, our Sovereign, how majestic is your name in all
> the earth! (Ps. 8:3-4, 9)

In David's great repentance psalm, he adds,

> Going through the motions doesn't please you,
>   a flawless performance is nothing to you.
> I learned God-worship
>   when my pride was shattered.
> Heart-shattered lives ready for love
>   don't for a moment escape God's notice.
>
> (Ps. 51:16-17; *The Message*)

Worship, then, is not primarily the mechanics; it's the integrity of people engaging God in a relationship. Once again hear the psalmist:

> My question: What are God-worshipers like?
> Your answer: Arrows aimed at God's bulls-eye.
> God-friendship is for God-worshipers;
> They are the ones he confides in.
>
> (Ps. 25:12,14; *The Message*)

Spirit-led

Once it is clearly understood that worship is first of all an attitude in which a person embraces God as Number One, it is then right to juxtapose that attitude with actions—tangible expressions—which will fortify and expand that attitude. This can only happen from a human standpoint when people are Spirit-led. We need to understand that in the Old Testament God gave specific instructions about what to do, but in the New Testament Jesus Christ fulfills all of those regulations. The woman at the well tried to get Jesus sidetracked by bringing up the details of worship: "Our ancestors worshiped on this mountain, but you say that the place where people must worship is in Jerusalem." Jesus, however, abruptly refocused the discussion on the spirit of worship:

> Woman, believe me, the hour is coming when you will worship the Father neither on this mountain nor in Jerusalem...the hour is coming, and is now here, when the true worshipers will worship the Father in spirit and truth, for the Father seeks such as these to worship him. God is spirit, and those who worship him must worship in spirit and truth (John 4:20-24).

Imagine two worshipers. One is a man in a contemporary praise service with his hands up in the air and the second is a woman in a liturgical church making the sign of the cross as she kneels before a big gold altar with a cross in the background. The question is, which best portrays worship? The answer is, "neither or both." This matches the Old Testament point that humans "look on the outward appearance, but the LORD looks on the heart" (1 Sam. 16:7).

There are at least two legitimate reasons for this. First, only God can truly see a human heart. Second, humans easily focus on outward appearance because we cannot help but live in a material world which we experience through the physical senses of touch, smell, taste, sight, and sound. To expand that a bit, humanity encompasses body, mind and emotion. All those things will inevitably come into focus in our worship, and yet those things must always be subservient to "heart" (or being people of the Spirit).

Good worship, then, is grounded in both truth (God-honoring) and experience (Spirit-led). Good worship exalts God as God in all the greatness and grandeur, glory and majesty which so quickly goes beyond our ability to comprehend, and it also embraces an attitude that humbly confesses our own humanity as finite, sinful, and needy in the presence of the Creator-Redeemer God. Several descriptions of Brethren in Christ worship will quickly illustrate the point.

When the Brethren in Christ congregation at Begumphur, India, meets for worship, the worshipers walk to the small one-room church from their nearby village. People remove their shoes at the door of the church in a sign of respect and proceeded to their seats on the floor, sitting cross-legged for the entire two-hour service. Men sit on one side, women on the other; children sit in the front rows, adults toward the middle and rear of the room. A row of men serve as musicians (since women do not generally play instruments), accompanying the congregation on the harmonium (a bellows-powered keyboard instrument), drums, cymbals, kabkubi (a plucked single-stringed instrument), and loud metal rattles. Although their facial expressions seem rather stoic, everyone sings with enthusiasm, clapping loudly. The songs are sung from memory; only a few people have hymnals and there are no overhead projectors. The few chairs are reserved for church leaders and visitors. The pastor typically leads the congregation through a rather straightforward exegesis of the morning Scripture, expounding on each verse of the passage. A clear hierarchy of leadership and an obvious division by gender prevail throughout the service.

The Harvest Community Church meets near Maytown, Pennsylvania, at a local school for worship. Two and a half hours before the service, volunteers set up the room. Announcements precede the service, projected on a screen while recorded music plays in the background. The "worship team," comprised of several singers and instrumental accompanists (including electronic keyboard player, guitarists and drummer), opens the service with a welcome. They then lead the congregation in 20-25 minutes of song interspersed with Scripture, commentary and prayer. The congregation usually stands during the singing time, sometimes clapping along, sometimes raising their hands in the air. Words for the songs are projected on a screen at the front of the room. The pastor, dressed in a pullover sweater, delivers his sermon from behind a music stand. The pastor uses a full manuscript, but delivery is fairly informal with ample illustrations and practical applications. Children remain in the service for the first half, leaving thereafter for a time of teaching and small group activity.

When the Brethren in Christ congregation at Grantham, Pennsylvania, meets for worship, a prelude of pipe organ music precedes the service. Worship begins with opening words from one of the pastoral staff, usually followed by a strong traditional hymn from the hymnal, led and accompanied by the organ. The bulletin provides a detailed order of worship to guide the congregation through each facet of the service. Included in the worship is singing (without hand clapping), Scripture reading (responsive and otherwise), prayers and offerings. Special music is usually provided by a choir dressed in choir robes and seated at the rear of the platform. The senior pastor and others involved in leading worship "dress up" for the occasion. The pastor delivers the morning sermon in an engaging and comfortable manner, following a manuscript written out word for word.

Which of these would we say was good worship? Indeed, what do we mean when we talk about "good" worship? The answer can cover any number of outward forms from spontaneous to liturgical, from traditional to contemporary, from western to non-western. But all outward forms must be grounded in what God has said and done if there is to be "good" worship; and at the same time, any worship is "good"—regardless of external form—if Jesus is honored and the presence of his Spirit is a reality in the hearts of the worshipers. So, yes, we value "heartfelt worship that is both God-honoring and Spirit-led," but that does not prescribe any certain outward form. Likewise, we must always insist that good worship has its context in the presence of God as mediated by Jesus and enabled by his Spirit.

Life-changing

A third dimension of worship that is valued by the Brethren in Christ is "life-changing." The lines are not so clear here. The basis of a changed (and changing) life is God's total gift of salvation (see chapter one). Our worship of God flows out of our reception of that life-changing gift. At the same time, worship is itself an integral facet of the life-giving power of God. It is in worship that we discover more and more of who God is and what our relationship with him means. Worship is the intersection of God's Spirit meeting with us, whose own spirits have been brought to life, so that something of a spiritual "fusion" occurs. It is impossible to so meet and interface with the Spirit of God without being changed.

God's people being affected by worship is explicitly illustrated in the Scriptures. Isaiah became acutely aware of his own sin as he was pulled into God's majesty in his vision of the heavenly throne, with celestial creatures chanting the refrain of God's holiness (Isa. 6). David danced before the ark in his hilarity of God's faithfulness and strength (2 Sam. 6:1-5). And John, the disciple that was closest to Jesus on earth, was prostrate before the splendor of the risen Christ (Rev. 1:9-20). In these and other examples, the Bible demonstrates that genuine worship leads to a profound transformation.

Summary

Good worship—the kind of worship we want to value—needs to have a healthy integration of these three factors. Worship needs to first of all have what we might call substance. This is the most basic part of worship: the fact that worship is focused on God and needs to be faithful to what is true about God. This is the essence of "God-honoring." Worship is also integrally connected to those who are doing the worshiping. If God is the object of worship, worshipers are the subjects. There is no worship without a God to be adored, but neither is there worship without beings to adore him. The way this happens is through and by the activity of the Holy Spirit, so worship is "Spirit-led." Finally, when worshipers are thrust into the manifest presence of God through the activity of the Spirit, there will be "life-changing" results. This is exactly what God offers and intends in this activity called worship. In worship we come in contact with the Creator-Redeemer God; the one before whose presence all the heavenly creatures can only bow and say "Holy, holy, holy, the Lord God the Almighty" (Rev. 4:8)!

The Boundaries of Worship

If our concerns stopped here, we could avert the angst and arguments that are so often connected to a discussion of worship. However, the limitations of humanity often mean that we try to limit worship to our understandings of God and our experiences in the Spirit. It is when the worship of God is restricted by human limitations that worship quickly becomes less than it can and should be.

To have worship that is "God-honoring, Spirit-led and life-changing," the essence or substance of worship only needs to fall within certain boundaries, and those boundaries can be as broad as God himself. Likewise, boundaries which do not embrace the full spectrum of the complexities of humanity are going to fall short of the glory of God and create divisiveness within the body of Christ. Whatever falls within those appropriate boundaries can be "good worship." As long as God is honored, the Spirit is directing his people, and lives are being changed (to be like Jesus), there is "good" worship. What are some boundaries for good worship? We want to identify four.

Biblical Truth

First, there is the boundary of biblical truth. The focus of worship is God the Father, Son, and Holy Spirit as he has revealed himself in the Scriptures. Obviously, not all Christians understand all the details of the Bible the same way, but there is a generally agreed upon orthodoxy which can help define Christian worship. Beyond that, it is inevitable that biblical distinctives will also have an influence within each theological tradition.

All Christians come to the Bible with a tradition of biblical interpretation. Sometimes the emphasis is as much or more on the tradition than the Bible itself. One strand of Brethren in Christ tradition is Anabaptism, which, among other things, was a restorative movement in church history that sought to "restore" the purity of the New Testament Church (see the Introduction). While the Old Testament is rich in worship imagery using various musical instruments (and dance!), the New Testament makes reference only to the human voice. This literal application of the New Testament led to the a capella tradition among Brethren in Christ people until the "accommodation" decision in the 1950s when musical instruments entered the church.

The point here is not whether instrumentation for worship is actually right or wrong, or even whether or not "restoration" efforts are valid. Rather, the point is that different Christian traditions can claim (with all sincerity) "biblical" reasons for their positions without being able to see that the Bible does not give unilateral support for many of the practices a particular tradition may hold dear.

At the same time, any group of believers that takes the Scriptures seriously will certainly attempt a degree of biblicism. A too-limited understanding of the Bible breeds pride of one's own position, fear of those who are different, and thus, sectarianism. An understanding of biblical truth which is too expansive will create a people who do not know how to exercise conviction on issues which are truly important. It seems to be difficult for Christians to humbly hold convictions; either the humility or the conviction is easily compromised in lieu of the other. In the context of worship, we either think everyone should worship like us (because we are "biblical"), or we give up having any commonality in worship while hoping that we maintain an integrating identity through other issues. Between these two extremes is an expansive range of worship choices that can have the full support of being "biblical."

Tradition

This brings up the second boundary, which is tradition. Notice we are not saying that tradition (or history) by itself should define worship. We are saying, however, that history and tradition should influence worship. This is to say that we believe the Holy Spirit has been at work throughout the life of the church, and some things that God's people have found to be helpful across the centuries should be studied and used. We say "studied" because their usefulness might not at first be apparent. But there are reasons some things have withstood the test of time, and it is wise to understand what those are and why.

It is all too easy to be short-sighted and think only of ourselves (our own context, our own theology, our own tastes) in the context of worship. The Bible presents worship as an activity which spans both the seen and unseen worlds and extends past the boundary of immediacy. The Te Deum reminds us that our worship joins voices with angels and cherubs and seraphs, prophets and apostles and martyrs who are around God's throne. Our worship is in continuity with the worship of God's people who have gone before us. We need a boundary of history and tradition to keep us aware of this.

We will suffer from self-imposed impoverishment if we ignore expressions of the faith which were distilled in the great creeds of the early church. There are great hymn texts which have earned a place in the church because they have endured after one hundred, five hundred, or even a thousand years. To reject these things because they sound outdated to modern ears can cause destructive spiritual pride. There is an inherent haughtiness in any practice that would dismiss the past in favor of only a contemporary spirituality.

Relevancy

The third boundary might seem contradictory to what we have just said, but it should be understood as complementary. This is the boundary of time and place, which can be captured in the popular word "contemporary," or perhaps this is a legitimate place for the word "relevant." There is a reason why the Bible is not read in Hebrew or Greek in our worship services, just as there is a reason why the worship service has not been frozen in the Latin of much of the early church: no one would understand since most of us only speak and understand English. The Christian gospel is not time- or culture-bound. Christian faith is adaptive. People in ancient Rome, people in Germany during the Middle Ages, people in America in the twenty-first century, and people living in the Amazon jungle as though it were still the Stone Age can all worship God through Jesus Christ. The worship will not look or sound the same in its detail, but it can be true worship. Even as we give God all we are, we give him who we are. What we offer God in the context of this denomination is a collection of people who are mostly middle-class white Americans living at the turn of the third millennium since Christ. This is a descriptive reality which begs questions of strategic approach and direction for the future. It is appropriate and right for us to desire greater demographic diversity. At the same time, who we are now cannot help but establish a boundary to our worship.

Style

There is a fourth boundary, but it should be the least consequential. Unfortunately, it seems to get the most attention. This fourth boundary is what we have called style. It goes beyond the issues of time and place, since any number of people in a contemporary setting can have a broad diversity of styles. However, style does affect us. It can have an overwhelming influence on where we choose to worship. Style quickly takes us to the issue of personal taste. It is certainly appropriate that we each have and understand our respective tastes in worship. In fact, whole congregations will likely have characteristics which are shaped by the stylistic preferences and tastes of their people. This kind of identity both shapes and is shaped by the other external forms that define our existence. At the same time, we need to exercise ongoing care that style and taste are not mistaken for what can be termed the "essence" of worship.

Being human, we will always be pulled to what is externally visible. That is what we so easily "sense." It is passion for external forms that mostly compels our discussions (arguments?) and motivates our own pleasure or displeasure. However, our passion for forms should not dictate our feelings about the quality of our worship. At the same time, we cannot operate separate from external forms; any human expression requires them. Among these are cultural expectations, designs, mechanisms, and materials. Under these categories are such practical options as: simple or complex, formal or informal, participatory or performance-dominated, spontaneous or planned, cognitive or emotive, old or new. The truth is, any of these can be "God-honoring, Spirit-led and life-changing." It is important for those who lead the church in worship to understand why.

For example, it would be easy for some people to negatively equate country-gospel music with a lack of sophistication, hymnody with an unhealthy degree of cognition, drum sets with an undesirable link either to secularism or primitivism, and classical music to elitism. These attitudes are not based in any inherent nature of style and instrument, but rather in associations that exist because of cultural context and history.

One of the biggest issues with style is the songs used in worship. Some songs are written to direct the worshiper toward the bigness of God. Likewise, other songs flow out of the reality of human experience. "Heartfelt worship" demands both. In the current debate between stereotypical hymns and choruses, it is important to recognize that both are really "worship songs." Both hymns (so-called) and choruses (so-called) have strong and weak examples of "good worship music."

Or, consider the effect of the "order of worship." Any corporate worship will have a tangible shape. It has been our observation that some individuals, some congregations, and indeed some cultures prefer (and perhaps need) different worship orders. The more subdued person could prefer a worship order that has relatively little demonstrative movement. The more intense people among us may prefer a worship order that models unfettered exuberance. Any given onlooker might say the former service is "too cold," or that the latter is "too emotional." In neither case is the onlooker looking at the heart of the worshipers. Both worship orders have attributes that appeal to certain personal or group preferences.

As an example in this context of order, the use of bulletins can be an issue that gets confused with worship itself, positively or negatively. The mechanism of a bulletin can serve to orient and direct participants as they worship. Conversely, the need for variety and a certain degree of spontaneity leads many individuals and congregations to become impatient with mechanisms like bulletins that seem to confine worship unduly. But the issue extends far beyond the one illustration of bulletins. Other mechanisms one might consider include the use of a song leader, the manner in which announcements are made in a worship service, or the extent to which (or what kind of) technology is used. Each of these mechanisms can affect people's thoughts and experiences of worship.

It is easy to attach stereotypical connections with mechanisms, thus limiting their use in worship. This is precisely the situation with the organ and the drum set. Each instrument is merely a mechanism (or a vehicle) for expressing music. In the hands of a skilled player, an organ is perfectly able to accompany contemporary songs. There is no musical reason to keep it from doing so. Anyone with an acquaintance with black gospel music knows how central the organ is to this musical style and how close black gospel music is to the pop music of our time. Similarly, there is no inherent musical conflict between a drum set and traditional hymnody. In the hands of a skilled player, the drums are perfectly able to accompany traditional hymns. One is making a flawed distinction when there is an attempt to draw inherent qualitative differences between the drum set of a typical rock band and the percussion section of a symphony orchestra. Like the organ, the modern drum set merely attempts to bring together a variety of individual instruments in the hands (and feet) of a single player. The overly-strong connections we have made with specific styles are what inhibit our use of these instruments across stylistic categories.

So, in the quest to have good materials for worship, the issue is far greater than style and taste. Are we able to recognize forms which bring us into the reality of God's presence? And can we admit that the same external forms do not work the same for everyone? Traditional hymns may not work in some settings or with certain groups of people; contemporary songs may not work in others; and both may be inappropriate for non-western settings. It is ironic to note, parenthetically, that more than one hundred years after the inappropriate introduction of Euro-American-styled hymnody to Africa, American missionaries have begun to export North American praise songs to non-western settings. These missionaries evidently assume that praise songs are somehow culturally neutral and therefore appropriate anywhere. The human needs and manifestations of worship are unavoidable, but it remains that the essence of Christian worship is any context where God and his people "connect."

Conclusion

The bottom line is this: worship is an attitude we embrace, individually and corporately, before the God of the Ages who has acted on our behalf through the life, death and resurrection of his Son. Anything called worship which does not draw attention to that and give honor to that is not worship. Worship brings us into the presence of the living God, who has revealed himself to us so that he can save us. He saves us by coming into our lives in order to remake us into the likeness of his Son, Jesus. Worship that is true and good will change us so that we are increasingly identifying with who God is. That is the essence of worship. To that end, we in the Brethren in Christ Church value heartfelt worship that is God-honoring, Spirit-directed, and life-changing.

Discussion Questions

1. What personal life experiences have shaped your understanding and expectations of worship?

2. What contributes to "good" worship? Does God have a preference for one style of worship over another or for one instrument over another?

3. What ought the balance be between history or tradition and contemporary relevancy?

4. What should Brethren in Christ worship look like? Should Brethren in Christ worship in Southern California look and sound like Brethren in Christ worship in Lancaster or Miami?

5. To what extent should we export North American worship style to the rest of the world?

6. What are some implications for Christian worship as the world increasingly becomes a global village? What might the Latin Church offer Euro-American worship and vice versa?

7. Using the following polarities, chart your own worship preference:
   simple—complex
   formal—informal
   participatory—performance dominated
   spontaneous—planned
   cognitive—emotive
   traditional—contemporary

8. What are some of the more prominent external forms that are affecting worship today and what are the pros and cons for these forms? How might worship conflict with popularity and cultural relevancy?

9. Do we care if we can no longer worship together as a denomination because our styles, forms and repertories are so different?

10. What elements of worship might unite Brethren in Christ congregations?

For Further Reading

Cymbala, Jim. *Fresh Wind, Fresh Fire*, Grand Rapids, Mich.: Zondervan Publishing House, 1997.

Hustad, Donald P. *True Worship: Reclaiming the Wonder and Majesty*. Wheaton, Ill.: Harold Shaw Publishers, Hope Publishing Company, 1998.

Liesch, Barry. *The New Worship: Straight Talk on Music and the Church*. Grand Rapids, Mich: Baker Books, 1996.

Morgenthaler, Sally. *Worship Evangelism: Inviting Unbelievers into the Presence of God*. Grand Rapids, Mich.: Zondervan Publishing House, 1995.

Webber, Robert E. *Blended Worship: Achieving Substance and Relevance in Worship*. Peabody, Mass.: Hendrickson Publishers, 1996.

4

Following Jesus

*We value wholehearted obedience
to Christ Jesus through the
empowering presence of the Holy Spirit.*

by Harvey Sider

*The narrow gate is obedience.... The broad gate is
simply doing whatever I want to do.*[1]
–Dallas Willard

Imagine yourself standing in line at McDonald's. Someone taps you from behind, and with an authoritative but gentle voice says, "Follow me." Questions flood your mind as you glance around to see the intruder. Why should I obey a stranger? Why should I leave my profession for something totally unknown? Where will this lead? What will my friends think? What kind of success will come from such a move? What may this mean for my family, community, and business involvements?

Jesus' first words to Peter challenged him to "Come, follow me" (Mark 1:17). Likewise, his final words, "Follow me!", emphatically reminded Peter that his call to obedience was personal and total (John 21:22). Sandwiched between these first and last words to Peter were three years for him to follow Jesus. It was an opportunity for him to observe carefully the priorities and practices of Jesus, to learn from word and deed, and to begin to understand the importance of obedience to the lordship of Christ and his new kingdom values. No longer could Peter merely fulfill his own personal goals or selfish whims. Rather, being a disciple would involve wholehearted obedience to Christ Jesus through the empowering presence of the Holy Spirit.

Following Jesus Involves Learning, Growing, and Obeying

Living in India for over a decade enabled me to better comprehend the implications of following a leader. I was always fascinated as I watched the common scene of a "guru" (holy man) with his "chela" (disciple). Without any protestations or questions, the disciple literally followed the master wherever he went—to the icy mountaintop or hot dusty desert, into the concrete jungles of huge cities like Calcutta or the villages of the countryside. No matter how severe the location or commonplace the order, the follower obeyed every command, even attempting to anticipate the unspoken desire of the guru.

As I observed the close and growing relationship between two such people, three essential aspects emerged. First, following required a willingness on the student's part to learn from the master and to have his own thinking remolded. Second, the disciple constantly developed new patterns of living. Above all, the follower completely obeyed the master. Without arguing, the student simply obeyed instructions. In much the same way, following Jesus is a call to learn, develop new patterns of living, and to obey his will completely.

A Call To Learn

At the beginning of his ministry, Jesus introduced his listeners to a curriculum that was totally different from anything they had ever encountered. In the Sermon on the Mount (Matt. 5–7), Jesus articulated foundational principles for them to follow. During the next three years, Jesus' teachings and example reinforced and enlarged on these important principles. As a result, the disciples began a journey that took them on a new learning curve, a journey along which Jesus shared with them the implications of the master/student relationship. As we explore some of these teachings, the fuller impact of following Jesus becomes increasingly clear.

The Beatitudes (Matt. 5:3-12) portray persons who have submitted themselves to Jesus Christ and who have learned the meaning of a new relationship. This relationship involves being vitally attached to God and subjected to the counter-cultural values of his kingdom, and it requires an entirely new approach to living. To lose oneself and to rest in the Creator Savior and his kingdom principles is to experience a deep sense of satisfaction, peace and shalom (wholeness) that extends beyond the circumstances of life. Abiding and deep-rooted joy are anchored in Christ and in loving, humble relations with each other.

In the Beatitudes, Jesus identifies various characteristics or values which, though seemingly upside down in today's world, are actually "right side up" for his followers. In recounting these instructions, Matthew notes the teacher/student connection that existed between Jesus and his disciples (5:1-2). What Jesus desires the "learner" to grasp is revolutionary.

Jesus announces, for example, that those who recognize their spiritual poverty and disconnectedness from God become candidates for the reign of God in their hearts and lives (5:3). His followers will likewise experience comfort in the Lord, regardless of the nature and extent of their sorrow (5:4). All told, Jesus extols such things as meekness (a blend of gentleness and strength), a thirst for God and what is right, mercy, purity, peacemaking, and commitment to God under pressure. In so doing, he calls his followers to learn an entirely new set of values; values that transform how we act at home, in the church, and in the world. As we shall see later, however, it is only by an act of intentional obedience, empowered by the Holy Spirit, that Christians are able to live this countercultural way.

A Call to Develop New Patterns of Living

In this opening message, Christ also calls his listeners to something more than a different form of religion, since external practices may be superficial and even hypocritical. For followers of Christ, inner thoughts and even attitudes take on great importance. As a result, anger, lust, and greed are to be replaced with forgiveness (Matt. 5:21-26, 38-48), purity (5:27-32), and generosity (5:42). Likewise, such activities as prayer, fasting, and giving to the needy must not be performed for show or personal benefit. Obedience to Jesus involves living a Christlike life (Matt. 6:1-8).

Jesus' challenge to his followers strikes at both the heart and the mind, the very sources which drive us to act as we do (Matt. 15:11, 17-20). Those whose inner lives have been transformed strive to live holy lives, whether the matter is public or private. In *First Hand Faith*, Bruce Wilkinson tells the unfortunate story of over two thousand Christian leaders who had attended a Christian convention in a major hotel. Upon checkout, the hotel administrator shared his surprise that more than half those delegates had watched X-rated videos while at the Conference.[2]

The issues may vary from place to place, of course, depending on our circumstances. We must apply lifestyle discipleship to the culture in which we live. Appianda Arthur, former member of the Ghanian Parliament and an organizer of the recent First International Consultation on Discipleship held in England in 1998, said it well when he reminded the group:

> In Africa, the key issues for discipleship may include bribery, corruption, and polygamy. In the West, you might want to focus on hedonism and materialism. The subjects change, but the core need is the same—discipleship.[3]

Christ continues this first message to his followers by addressing our relationship to money and possessions (Matt. 6:19-34). Living in a world where consumerism and materialism are extremely important, Christians must constantly beware of what takes priority in life: money, things, pleasure, or God. Jesus stresses that the disciple is to trust God rather than material wealth. Following Christ means that our wealth should accumulate in heaven rather than on earth. Shockingly, he calls those who follow the path of seeking prosperity "pagans" or "gentiles" and reminds his followers that it is impossible to serve both God and money (6:32). Is there a chance we have been trapped in what Mark Buchanan aptly calls "the Cult of the Next Thing"? According to Buchanan,

> Those caught up in the Cult of the Next Thing live endlessly, relentlessly for, well, the Next Thing—the next weekend, the next vacation, the next purchase, the next experience. For us, the impulse to seek the Next Thing is an instinct bred into us so young it seems genetic.[4]

As followers of Jesus we are called to new patterns of living in which our priorities center on the eternal rather than the material.

A Call to Complete Obedience

In Matthew 7:13-14, Jesus instructs his listeners to enter through the narrow gate; for the gate is wide and the road is easy that leads to destruction, and there are many who take it. For the gate is narrow and the road is hard that leads to life, and there are few who find it.

Too often readers of the Bible apply these key verses in Jesus' sermon to the initial choice one makes when becoming a Christian. While such an application is understandable, the primary focus of the verse within the context of the sermon is on obedience. As Dallas Willard reminds us in *The Divine Conspiracy*, to do the will of God is to walk the narrow road rather than doing whatever we want.[5] This carries the Christian beyond the initial joy and freedom of new life in Jesus. The narrow gate involves a walk with the Lord, wherever it leads and whatever the cost.

Both the Old and New Testaments emphasize the necessity of obedience as we walk with the Lord. In addition to the many Old Testament passages in which the people of Israel are instructed to obey the Lord (i.e., Exod. 19:5; Deut. 5:1; 6:25; Josh. 1:7), various "obedient" people appear as examples to follow. Two such individuals are Abraham and Samuel.

After waiting a lifetime for a promised son, God asked Abraham to do an unlikely and seemingly unreasonable thing—offer his only and long-anticipated child as a sacrifice. While it is impossible to know the thoughts that no doubt flooded Abraham's mind, he expressed his willingness to follow God's order by taking his son, Isaac, to the place of sacrifice, binding him, laying him on the altar, and then lifting the knife to kill him (Gen. 22:1-19). Graciously, God provided a substitute sacrifice.

Later, just after his coronation as King of Israel, Saul began to develop a pattern of self-service, doing what he wanted to do rather than obeying God. Finally, God called the prophet Samuel to confront King Saul for his disobedience. Swaggering Saul tried to ingratiate himself with Samuel and then to argue, but Samuel was steadfastly obedient in proclaiming to Saul the consequences of his wayward actions. To clinch his word, Samuel finally replied to Saul that the Lord was pleased and satisfied with complete obedience, not with all the external things that one may do to try to gain divine favor (1 Sam. 15:22-23).

In the New Testament, obedience remains a dominant theme. Jesus said to his followers, "If you love me, you will keep my commandments" (John 14:15). Many of them did. The tax collector Levi "got up and followed him" (Mark 2:14) as soon as Jesus called. It seems as if he did not even take time to complete his accounting records for the day! The recurring phrase "and immediately" (Matt. 4:20; Mark 1:18, 20) indicates an unquestioned willingness to follow Jesus. In all the gospels such comments emphasize that the disciples eagerly followed, whether to provide food for the multitudes or embark on a missionary journey. Their commitment was so wholehearted that, regardless of their vocation, they became fully engrossed in doing what the Lord said.

In the book of Acts, similar examples appear. Jesus' followers wait for the promised Holy Spirit (ch. 1), begin to evangelize their home turf (ch. 2), preach and heal (ch. 3), resist the fear tactics of the authorities (ch. 4), and increasingly move into cross-cultural and transnational ministry (chs. 4ff.). Chapter after chapter reveals the early Christians giving unquestioned obedience to the will of Christ.

Following Jesus in full obedience gives him highest priority in all of life. While this has endless implications, broad areas often affected include vocation, interpersonal relationships, time, and talents.

Obedience and Vocation

With respect to vocation, obeying God involves *doing* what he wants me to do *wherever* he wants me to do it. In his book, *The Cost of Discipleship*, Dietrich Bonhoeffer proclaimed, "It is not for us to choose which way we shall follow. That depends on the will of Christ."[6] Bonhoeffer actually paid the ultimate price for following Christ by being martyred by the Nazis for practicing obedience to the call of true discipleship.

For some, obedience may mean leaving a physical location or changing an occupation. After eight satisfying, successful and fulfilling years as an elementary teacher and principal, I joyfully followed Christ in a different direction. To dissuade me from such a move, the superintendent of schools offered me the principalship of the largest school in the county. I'm glad I declined! Later, while serving as a pastor at a mission church, (now the Bridlewood Brethren in Christ Church in Toronto), I began to consider a call to serve in India. One elderly man, who was not a member of the church, said to me, "Why would you waste your life in such a dark and backward country?"

Numerous lay people have responded and continue to obey the call of Christ by relocating and sometimes taking up a different vocation in order to be available where needed. Church planting and overseas ministries often seek out and encourage lay people to relocate to help build Christ's Kingdom. Teachers, doctors, computer technicians, farmers, nurses, pastors, those with trades, and many others have given and are continuing to give significantly of some of the most meaningful and productive years of their lives as they obediently serve in new locations. The journey of discipleship is one of following wherever the Lord calls. Such a call is no respecter of either vocation or location.

Benjamin Marandi of India stands as a shining example of one whose priority in life was Jesus Christ. There was an immediate attachment and total loyalty to Christ as soon as he renounced his practice as a well-known witch doctor. For several years he continued to live at home and follow his comfortable lifestyle, making a reasonable livelihood on his small farm. At the same time, he began to study the Bible diligently, with a special focus on the New Testament. When the Lord called him to relocate north of the Ganges River where the Brethren in Christ felt led to establish a work among the Santals, he responded immediately to an invitation that arrived through one of our churchmen, Isaac Paul. In fact, even though he was in the middle of harvest, the very next day Benjamin left the threshing floor and the remaining harvesting to his young son. He went with Isaac to begin a new work among his people, the Santals, who had not yet heard the gospel.

For Benjamin, obedience meant always being on the move from village to village, singing and witnessing in the midst of opposition and sometimes persecution, until a strong group of Christians emerged. He continued his itinerant evangelism even as he found it necessary to devote more time to discipling and shepherding this new body of believers. His compassion for people caused him to be constantly giving money, food, advice, and consolation. Whenever he had a few minutes of spare time, one could find him with the open Bible spread on the ground, worshiping the Lord and preparing to share what the Scriptures taught. Benjamin's attachment to Christ drove him to follow Jesus in ministry to others, regardless of great cost in living comfort and personal desires.

Obedience and Interpersonal Relationships

In terms of interpersonal relationships, complete obedience to Christ often involves new challenges and responsibilities. Throughout the Sermon on the Mount (Matt. 5–7), Jesus speaks of relating to spouses (5:27-32), enemies (5:43-48), and siblings (7:1-5). Essentially, Jesus calls his followers to reconcile differences and to love and care for all others, no matter who they may be. When personalities clash or when others seem to get their way, Christ's followers are called to love and forgive, and to work through tough issues. This is part of practicing complete obedience.

After Jesus, John and Paul expand significantly on his call to costly and complete obedience in our new relationships. In a way, John summarizes this by simply saying " we may be sure that we know him (Jesus), if we obey his commandments (1 John 2:3; cf. 2:6). He then repeatedly emphasizes the connection between obedience and love for others (i.e., 3:11-18; 4:7-12). Finally, as a "clincher," John boldly equates our love for God with our love for each other (5:2-3).

Paul addresses the same issue with even more specificity. For example, he tackles the explosive and divisive issue of church worship in various places and ways. In so doing, he intentionally situates the "love chapter" (1 Cor. 13) between his teachings on spiritual gifts (1 Cor. 12 and 14). In Ephesians and elsewhere, Paul calls for obedience in the give and take of confrontation and submission. All Christians are to "speak the truth in love," be kind and compassionate, forgiving one another (Eph. 4–5). These acts of obedient love are usually costly and tough, but they are a crucial dimension of living as a disciple of Christ.

Obedience, Time, and Talents

In addition to vocation and interpersonal relationships, obeying the Lord affects such things as our use of time and talents. Concerning time, all of us have responsibilities to fulfill and expectations to meet. But Christians need to examine how they spend their time, including moments of relaxation and renewal. Watching meaningless television programs, spending countless hours browsing the internet, going to questionable places and other kinds of wasteful leisure experiences are good indicators of the priority Jesus has in our lives. Often our time could be better used in the study of God's Word, relating to needy people physically, emotionally and spiritually, and in praise and adoration of the Lord.

In terms of talents, obedience calls us to surrender our abilities to serve Christ and others. Scripture repeatedly suggests that we have been gifted by God in order to serve each other (Rom. 12; 1 Cor. 12; Eph. 4:7-16). Our responsibility to use these gifts is highlighted in the story Jesus told of the three servants, one of whom refused to use his gift (Matt. 25:14-30). All three were "gifted" differently, but one felt limited and was unwilling to use his resources. In refusing to use his talent, he displayed disdain for both the gift and the giver, and in so doing became self-condemned. To refuse to use our "talent" squanders our abilities to minister and removes Jesus from the throne of our lives. Whether one is called and gifted to be a technician, teacher, farmer, doctor, lawyer, housewife, chef, pastor—the list seems endless—one's commitment to follow Christ implies that a person cultivates the skills for the building of the body (1 Cor. 12:7). While some gifts are more prominently displayed, each is equally important and necessary in the development of the church.

A life of obedience to Christ obviously comes at a very significant cost. The nature of such a cost will vary depending on many circumstances. For the rich young man, it was the giving up of his comfort, prestige and money. For him, the price was greater than he was willing to pay (Matt. 19:16-22). In some countries, following Christ literally means death or, at the very least, ostracization from family and friends. For everyone the term "self-denial" is appropriate. Many Scriptures insist that the road to obedience is one of self-denial. Jesus said "Whoever does not carry the cross and follow me cannot be my disciple" (Luke 14:27). In addition, "none of you can become my disciple if you do not give up all your possessions" (Luke 14:33). Finally, in Matthew 16:24, Jesus summarizes the principle in the clearest way possible: "If any want to become my followers, let them deny themselves and take up their cross and follow me."

In words written under the most difficult of circumstances, Bonhoeffer describes our relation to Christ this way: "When we are called to follow Christ, we are summoned to an exclusive attachment to his person."[7] When the early disciples responded to Jesus' call to follow, they discovered a new attachment, and it was to his person rather than the things around them. Following Jesus today brings with it the same call, establishing new priorities which only intentional and determined obedience can help us fulfill. But it is just that new attachment to Christ which influences us to rethink our priorities and obey his will. For Jesus and for us, such discipleship is at the very heart of the gospel.

The Holy Spirit Enables Us to Learn, Live, and Obey

After emphasizing the importance of discipleship, our core value identifies the driving force which enables to us live in "wholehearted obedience to Christ Jesus." Through his empowering presence, the Holy Spirit instructs us and leads us into all truth (John 16:12). He makes it possible to learn, live, and obey.

Learning

When Jesus, the master teacher, was spending his last hours with the disciples, he began to introduce them to their new teacher. Jesus understood that they would not learn God's way if left completely to themselves, so he devoted significant time to help his followers understand the ministry of the Holy Spirit. He began with the basic truth that the Holy Spirit would now become their instructor in the teacher/student relationship (John 14:26). The Holy Spirit will lead people to Jesus (John 15:26), convict them of sin (John 16:9-10), and guide them into truth (John 16:12). Then, taught by and empowered by the Spirit, the disciples will themselves teach others about the Spirit's work in their lives. In the limited context of this section, we will explore briefly the relationship of the Holy Spirit to believers and how the Spirit enables us to learn.

First, living in the Spirit includes more than a simple act of forgiveness of sins through Jesus Christ, a necessary and wonderful experience. While we sinners are transformed by the power of the Holy Spirit (Rom. 8:9), God wants us to move beyond this initial gift of salvation. So Paul calls us to "live by the Spirit," to be "led by the Spirit," and to be "guided by the Spirit" (Gal. 5:16-25). This means that Christians need to listen carefully so as to hear and be sensitive to the voice of the Spirit as he speaks through Scripture, circumstances, and our brothers and sisters. To develop such a life in the Spirit, there normally comes a time subsequent to the Spirit's conviction of sin and our birth into the kingdom of God, when we sense the need to surrender fully to the will of Jesus. At this point, a commitment must be made to allow the Spirit to guide and control every part of our lives. Ideally such an experience occurs soon after conversion. Personally, five years passed following my conversion before I understood enough and arrived at a place of full surrender to the Spirit's leading.

Second, the Holy Spirit teaches believers in a variety of ways. Using a basic educational principle, Jesus implies in the context of his teaching about the Holy Spirit that one must listen carefully to the voice of God (John 15–17). Later, speaking of church life, John emphasizes the same principle seven times through the words "listen to what the spirit is saying" (Rev. 2–3). Christians learn to the degree that they listen to the voice of the Holy Spirit. Therefore, the follower of Jesus must develop a willingness and a desire to listen, both in private and in corporate worship. By personal example as well as by word, Paul illustrated this principle. It was while waiting on the Spirit's direction that the church and Paul learned of the Spirit's desire to initiate the first missionary journey (Acts 13:1-3). Later, as Paul sought to discern direction for future ministry opportunities, the Spirit expressly closed and opened appropriate doors (Acts 16:6-10).

Living Differently

Because some of the implications of the empowering presence of the Holy Spirit have sometimes been misunderstood, several things must be kept in mind. First, Christians realize that freedom from the control of sin does not remove them from temptations or human desires. As long as the Lord gives life, we, like Christ, will always be subject to any of the temptations common to people. By living in the Spirit, however, we need not succumb to sin's enticements (1 Cor. 10:13). Additionally, it is essential that believers keep growing in grace and yielding to God's will. Finally, we must remain sensitive to the voice of the Holy Spirit and be quick to obey as he speaks to us through such avenues as the Scriptures, meditation, prayer, and other people in the church. While remaining free from the control of sin is not automatic, it is a provision made available for every Christian who lives in and walks by the enabling presence of the Holy Spirit.

When Christians live empowered by, and keep in step with the Spirit, they then can exhibit the fruit of love, peace, patience, kindness, goodness, faithfulness, gentleness, and self control (Gal. 5:2). My father accepted the challenge of being a bivocational church planter for a very small nucleus of Christians. His problems were numerous, almost from the beginning. One member of the group soon indicated that he, not my father, should be the leader. Then, the group attracted a few newcomers who were critical and had to be dealt with firmly. Some people grew dissatisfied with the worship style and left. Others began to attack various segments of my father's ministry, especially as he tried to reach the community for Christ. To make matters worse, the Great Depression left the emerging congregation feeling overwhelmed by the debt on the building. In spite of the host of problems and criticisms he faced, however, I never once heard him utter an unkind or critical word to or about any of his detractors. He simply continued to model and teach how the Spirit-filled life actually enabled one to live and produce the fruit of the Spirit.

Obeying

Jesus understood that the Holy Spirit would enable the disciples to obey him wholeheartedly. He therefore instructed them not to leave Jerusalem, but to wait for the gift of the Holy Spirit, saying, "you will receive power when the Holy Spirit has come upon you; and you will be my witnesses" (Acts 1:8). As they obediently waited, they were wonderfully rewarded (Acts 2:1-4). As a result of the Spirit's arrival, the previously fearful disciples had the courage and boldness to obey Jesus aggressively by living and proclaiming his message. They now obeyed Jesus' final command to preach the gospel in all the world and to make disciples (Matt. 28:19-20).

The entire book of Acts provides a marvelous case study of persons filled with the Holy Spirit obediently responding to the situation at hand. Peter seized the opportunity to preach boldly about Jesus on the day of Pentecost (Acts 2:14-36), sensed the need of the lame man and opened the way for Jesus to heal (3:1-10), spoke confidently in spite of threats (4:1-22), discerned and confronted evil (5:1-11), and established appropriate priorities for the believing community (6:1-6). Philip, under the prompting of the Spirit, left successful renewal meetings in Samaria to witness to a lone Ethiopian (8:29). It was the Holy Spirit who thrust the early church into cross-cultural ministries (chs. 10–11), and it was the same Spirit who initiated the great missionary journeys of Paul (13:2). During the months and years that followed, Paul constantly waited on the Spirit for his every move: when, where and how to preach boldly (13:4; 16:6); who to appoint as leaders for the new churches (20:28); and when to stand his ground and suffer the consequences rather than flee (20:23). In virtually every chapter of the book of Acts, the abiding presence of the Holy Spirit guided the early church.

The same must be true of Jesus' followers today. Once Christians have surrendered their wills and motives to the lordship of Christ, the Holy Spirit provides the power that enables them to be and do what Jesus taught. According to Paul's prayer for the church in Ephesians 3:14-21, the presence of the Spirit further helps believers to know Christ more intimately and to be filled with all the fullness of God. With such enablement, Christians have the desire and strength to live as obedient servants of Jesus. Without it, the call to discipleship is little more than wishful thinking.

Conclusion

As followers of Jesus Christ, we are called to learn, develop new patterns of living, and obey his will in all things. He is the master, and we are the disciples. To do this, we must be alert, sensitive, and obedient to the Spirit. Sometimes it is difficult to know what the Spirit may be trying to say and where he wants to lead us. However, as we live in the Spirit and cultivate communication with the Lord, we can be assured that our every step will be directed by God. As we fully surrender our lives to Christ, holding nothing in reserve, he guarantees us that the Holy Spirit will always enable us to meet every circumstance of life. To be a genuine Christian requires us to give wholehearted obedience to Jesus Christ through the empowering presence of the Holy Spirit. It is to walk the narrow way, placing what Jesus wants above our own wishes and ambitions.

Discussion Questions

1. Discuss the implications of likening Christian discipleship to a "guru" and his "chela." In what ways do you find this analogy helpful? What are its limitations?

2. Explore the phrase "complete obedience." Compare what such a phrase might mean in our culture. In other cultures.

3. What does it mean to "take up the cross" at home, school, and in our workplace? What struggles might we face in doing so?

4. Have you ever felt tension between obedience to Christ and your vocation? Has obedience to Christ ever prevented you from accepting a particular job? Has obedience to Christ ever led you into a new vocation?

5. How does obeying Christ affect your various interpersonal relationships? With your parents? Your spouse? Your siblings? Your neighbors? Your classmates?

6. In what ways does obeying Christ affect the way we utilize our talents? How might we discern between proper and improper uses of our talents?

7. What role does your church play in enabling you to be obedient and in holding you accountable? How can you be helpful to others as they seek to follow Christ?

8. Identify and discuss at least five specific areas where obedience has been a particular challenge for you. What makes these areas so challenging?

9. Discuss how obedience and sensitivity to the Holy Spirit affect the way we work at unity and servanthood in the church, home, and world.

10. Share a recent experience when you relied on the Holy Spirit for strength and direction. What did you learn from that experience that may assist you in obeying Christ in difficult times in the future?

For Further Reading

Bonhoeffer, Dietrich. *The Cost of Discipleship*. New York: Macmillan, 1953.

Foster, Richard. *Celebration of Discipline*. New York: Harper and Row, 1978.

Peterson, Eugene. *A Long Obedience in the Same Direction*. Downers Grove, Ill.: InterVarsity Press, 1980.

Willard, Dallas. *The Divine Conspiracy*. San Francisco: Harper-SanFrancisco, 1998.

Yancy, Philip. *The Jesus I Never Knew*. Grand Rapids: Zondervan, 1995.

5

Belonging to the Community of Faith

We value integrity in relationships and mutual accountability in an atmosphere of grace, love, and acceptance.

by Chuck Anderson

One of the rarest things in the cosmos is a soliton—
a chronically solitary particle which remains
unaffected even when it collides with another.
God only made a handful of solitons in the entire universe.
Humans are not one of them.[1]
—*Leonard Sweet*

When I was a child, my mother served as the accompanist in our local congregation. As a result, she dutifully towed me to church for every religious event imaginable—special music rehearsals, training union, revivals (*twice* a year), youth gatherings, and a seemingly endless array of meetings. I even missed the final ten minutes of Lassie every Sunday because they conflicted with choir practice!

Yet, despite all of this time spent under the steeple, only three memories clearly stand out as I think about my childhood church: (1) the day a guest evangelist claimed that the second coming of

Jesus would involve flying saucers (without question, the best sermon I heard as a child); (2) the great times I had playing on the front lawn of the church with my best friend, Mark, the pastor's son; and particularly (3) the night the church told Pastor Lassiter and his family to leave. I never learned all the details of what precipitated this firing. My mom told me it had something to do with selecting a church camp. Whatever the reason, I was crushed. It would be the only time I can ever remember crying in church as a child.

Ask many people today what comes to their minds when they think of church, and hopefully they will tell you beautiful stories of a place where their lives and the lives of others were forever changed through the merciful love of God and his people. For them, the church is a community of forgiven people who extend the love of God to a broken world. Yet, ask other people the same question, and they may well tell you a story similar to mine. For these people, the church has unfortunately become little more than a place where painful memories are born.

Given these differing evaluations, is there a path that will lead us to be the church that God truly desires? Can the church be a place where lost and hurting people come and find forgiveness, mercy and a "way back in"? As Brethren in Christ, we firmly believe so. For us, the church, not the state or any other identifiable group, is our primary community. Within it, we value integrity in relationships and mutual accountability in an atmosphere of grace, love, and acceptance.

The Hard Realities of Relationships

The Church of Jesus Christ will never be a place where people are perfect and problem-free. A poignant biblical reminder of this appears in Paul's public rebuke of Peter at Antioch (Gal. 2). On that occasion, Paul sensed that Peter was two-faced with regards to table fellowship with Gentiles. When Peter first arrived in Antioch, he freely ate with the Gentile believers there, showing no concern for their disregard of important Jewish dietary laws. However, with the arrival of a visiting delegation sent by James of Jerusalem, Peter stealthily withdrew (the word might be translated 'slithered') from the table and stopped dining with his Gentile brothers. Paul saw in Peter's behavior more than mere hypocrisy. For him, the fortune of the entire Gentile mission itself was a stake. If Peter's actions went unchallenged, the gospel would no longer have been based upon faith in Christ alone, but upon "works of the law" (vv. 15-21). Quickly, Paul rebuked Peter publicly, "before them all" (v. 14).

Concerned readers of the Bible might ask, "Did it really need to come to this?" "Did it *have* to be a public rebuke?" "Was there not a better way, a more 'Brethren in Christ' way for Paul to deal with the problem?" "Did Paul's actions violate the principle of graduated discipline spelled out by Jesus in Matthew 18:15-17?" And finally, "What was the ultimate outcome of this confrontation? Did Peter and Paul ever finally reconcile their broken relationship?"

So troubling was this story to the early church fathers that some finally concluded that the Peter of Galatians 2 could not be Peter the apostle. Some thought, "How is it possible for two great and holy men like Paul and Peter to disagree so strongly? This could not be Peter, the great apostle and pillar of the church!" Apparently, these fathers failed to appreciate one humbling reality about this young and developing church. As long as there are people in the church, there will always be problems in the church. Be they preferences in worship style, choices of carpet colors, decisions over church camps, personality conflicts, or more weighty theological disagreements—where people gather, problems must be expected.

The Hard Work of Relationships

Acknowledging the inevitability of problems, however, does not require us simply to accept them. In fact, the very inevitability of people-problems calls us to nurture fulfilling and lasting relationships. Developing such relationships in Christ demands hard work! As Henri Nouwen writes,

> Community is the place where the person you least want to live with always lives. Often we surround ourselves with the people we most want to live with, thus forming a club or a

clique, not a community. Anyone can form a club; it takes grace, shared vision, and hard work to form a community.[2]

Paul expresses a similar sentiment in a well-known but often misunderstood passage of Scripture:

> Therefore, my beloved, just as you have always obeyed me, not only in my presence, but much more now in my absence, work out your own salvation with fear and trembling; for it is God who is at work in you, enabling you both to will and to work for his good pleasure (Phil. 2:3-4).

But what does Paul mean when he instructs his listeners to "work out your own salvation"? What he does not mean is that people can be saved through an accumulation of their own good works. Just ask Peter about that—he learned his lesson the hard way! We know that salvation rests upon faith in Christ alone (see chapter one). Instead, the key to understanding this passage appears within Paul's previous and more comprehensive appeal for healthy relationships (Phil. 1:27; 2:1-5). There, Paul instructs the Philippian Christians to "do nothing from selfish ambition or conceit, but in humility to regard others as better than yourselves." Further, "Let each of you look not to your own interests, but to the interests of others" (2:3-4).

The "work" to which Paul refers, therefore, is the hard and difficult task of building, nurturing, and maintaining relationships as sisters and brothers in Christ. That this is in fact what the apostle had in mind receives final confirmation in 2:14-15, where he encourages the believers to "do all things without murmuring and arguing so that you may be blameless and innocent, children of God...." As Gordon Fee remarks, this text deals "with 'how saved people live out their salvation' in the context of the believing community and the world."[3] The inevitability of people-problems, once again, does not mean that we quietly accept or ignore them. Rather, our salvation calls us to work hard at forging meaningful personal relationships in Christ, even with difficult people.

Thankfully, the Scriptures help us in this important work by describing what redeemed relationships look like in practice. In general, three images or pictures of the church provide the parameters: (1) the People of God, (2) a Fellowship, and (3) the Body of Christ.

The Church as the People of God

One of the most beautiful descriptions of the church in the Bible is "God's people" (1 Peter 2:10). In this description, both the priority of people as well as the importance of modeling healthy relationships emerge.

The Priority of People and Relationships

The Brethren in Christ Core Value, *Belonging to a Community of Faith*, has as its most basic foundation one simple biblical principle. The Church is *a people*. At first glance this may appear straightforward enough. Yet there is a way in which dead religionism tends almost indiscernibly to hide such basic truths. Consider, for example, the common expression, "*go to church*." In one sense this brief phrase is innocent and seemingly harmless. The early disciples, however, would have scratched their heads upon hearing it. "How can one *go* to church?," they would have asked. "The church is not a place where someone goes. The church is a people." Biblically speaking, the only option before us is to *be* the church, not to *go* to one. When the church is seen primarily as a place, then *places* gain primary importance. But when the church is seen primarily as a people, then *people* become the focus.

The woman at the well, like most people of her day, was a person who was very much concerned about places. During a conversation with Jesus, she said, "Our ancestors worshiped on this mountain, but you say that the place where people must worship is in Jerusalem" (John 4:20). But Jesus would have none of that. Tall, holy mountains and sparkling, religious cities were not core values to him. As a result, he responded to her, not in terms of sacred places, but of sacred people: "the hour is coming, and is now here, when the true worshipers will worship the Father in spirit and truth, for the Father seeks such as these to worship him" (4:23). Clearly, the gospel is not about a God of places, but a God of people.

Because of this, churches must never allow *things* to take precedence over people. Church programs, building campaigns, and ecclesiastical extravaganzas are not the centers around which a church builds its existence. Too often, churches rely upon such things in order to sustain themselves. Typically, the only things sustained under such circumstances are the programs, campaigns, and events themselves. A far healthier approach, particularly at budget time, involves asking questions like, "What can we do this year that will build up our people and enhance their relationships?," "What can we accomplish this year that will bring our people into a more intimate relationship with God and with each other?," and "In what ways are the busyness and worthless demands of our church programs and structures working against the building of people-to-people relationships in Jesus Christ?" As John Havlik comments:

> The church is never a place but always a people;
> never a fold but always a flock;
> never a sacred building but always a believing assembly.
> The church is you who pray, not where you pray.
> A structure of brick and marble can no more be a church
> than your clothes of serge and satin can be you.
> There is in this world nothing sacred but man,
> no sanctuary of man but the soul. [4]

Describing the church as the people of God means first of all that, in the church, people are more important than places.

The Witness of Our Relationship

The second idea emphasized in this depiction of the church as "God's people" is the *witness* of our relationships. Our love for each other can have a profound impact on how the world around us sees and responds to God.

From the beginning, God desired to take for himself a people from among the nations of the world (Exod. 3:7). He therefore called Israel by his name (Exod. 3:15; cf. Jer. 14:9) and gave them his Law (Exod. 24). Rather than suppressing these chosen people, the Law provided guidelines and stipulations so that the Israelites could know the Lord and his ways (i.e., Gen. 49:29; Exod. 3:7, 10; Lev. 26:12). As a result, their lives and relationships were to reflect in visible and practical ways who God was (Exod, 9:16).

In the New Testament, the church is similarly viewed as God's people (Rom. 9:25; Titus 2:14; 1 Pet. 2:9-10). However, the Law is no longer written upon tablets of stone, but upon human hearts (Rom. 2:29). No longer living by "...*the old written code*" (Rom. 7:6), we have been sealed with the promised Holy Spirit who is working out God's purposes in us (2 Cor. 1:22; Eph. 1:13; 4:30). We, just as Israel of old, "*bear his name*" by the way in which we live out our lives and love one another (Acts 15:17; 1 Pet. 4:16). What other people see in us reflects in very visible and practical ways the nature and character of the God we serve. Thus, in the very act of loving one another, we witness for Christ.

Lost people today care very little about evangelistic verbiage. Hurting people are not impressed with mere words. According to Thomas Merton, "People don't want to hear any more words. In our mechanical age, all words have become alike. To say 'God is Love' is like saying, 'Eat Wheaties.'"[5] The world has had its fill of our religious Wheaties. What people are searching for is something that can nourish their lives, something real and wholesome. When we love one another and live out our calling as *the people of God*, the world will sit up, take notice and begin to get a glimpse of God.

Even though she had visited Grace Community only a few times, we all knew that Tina had some very real doubts about God. She never tried to cover them up. True seekers rarely do. Relationally open and honest, Tina quickly slipped into our hearts, living among us as a somewhat curious observer searching for something.

Tina was single and lived alone. Raised in an alcoholic's home and a recovering alcoholic herself, she had known a very troubled life. As a result, Tina found it extremely difficult to trust people, let alone God. She often raised an assortment of personal questions that reflected her struggles. "I've been rejected all my life. I must not be worth much to anyone. How is it that a God would ever be interested in me?" "People have let me down all my life. People let me down every day. Why would I ever want to depend upon God?" "How can I confide my struggles and my fears to a God I cannot see when I cannot even confide in people plainly visible and closest to me?" "How can I believe in a God who is supposed to be love when all I have ever seen are people who exhibit nothing but hate?" Such thoughts and concerns plagued her mind.

During the altar time one Sunday morning, Tina caught my eye from where she was seated. I could tell something was churning in her heart. She stood to her feet and quietly made her way to me at the platform. Clasping her hands in mine, she whispered to me, "Chuck, I feel I've got to tell you something right now. I hope you won't be too upset with me."

"Sure, Tina," I said. "It's OK. Tell me what's on your heart."

"I think I may like it here at Grace Community," she continued. "You guys seem genuine. You appear to love and care for each other. I feel I may be able to be vulnerable here with my fears and hurts. And I love the music. I love all the singing. I *really* like it here with you guys."

"Wonderful, Tina. That's great!" I said. "We know God has brought you here and we're glad he did."

"But Pastor Chuck," she continued, "I do have one *very* big problem with Grace."

"Oh? Let's talk about it, Tina," I said. "What's going on?"

"Well, it has to do with this, uh, *Jesus* thing. I still have a problem with this *Jesus* stuff. You guys are always talking about *Jesus* this and *Jesus* that. I just can't bring myself to believe in God. I can't believe all this matter about Jesus dying for me…loving me, knowing me, wanting me. I really would like to believe it all. I really *want* to believe it. But I just can't."

"Tina," I answered, "I want you to know how proud I am of you. Jesus doesn't mind all of these doubts you're carrying. Where you are right now—right up here this morning with all your concerns and all your questions—this is right where God wants you. You keep searching for him. We'll keep loving you. And in time, I know what's going to happen, Tina."

"What's that?" she asked.

I just smiled.

How exciting it was in the months that followed to watch God creatively pour his love into her life through the relational love of believers. Tina became even more deeply involved and connected with the people and families of the church. On Fridays and Saturdays she ate out, shopped, and just had fun with the other singles. She came regularly to all of the services to receive guidance and encouragement. One family in particular took Tina under its wings and prayed daily for her. They were there for her whenever she needed anything. Tina also attended every Bible study, energetically prepared with practical questions about the problems she had encountered during the week. No one took these questions defensively, and no one scolded her for being a nuisance. For the people of Grace Community, Tina was a gift from God.

It was at the Annual Women's Retreat that year where God forever resolved the *Jesus thing* for Tina. On that divinely orchestrated occasion, while among loving friends, Tina finally turned over her doubts and her heart to Jesus Christ. Today, she is a real trophy of God's love. A faithful and committed leader on the Grace Community Church worship team, Tina herself now leads her own weekly Bible study of a dozen women who are themselves seeking more of this *Jesus thing*.

One can only guess how many people there are in the world today whose problem with this *Jesus* thing is really far more a problem with this *church* thing. Our witness for God and our relationships with one another are inseparably linked. Perhaps the greatest investment we can make in evangelism is to take seriously this business of loving and accepting each other.

The Church as Fellowship

In the New Testament, the word *fellowship* refers to two things. First, it speaks of the communion that all Christians have with both Jesus (1 Cor. 1:9) and the Holy Spirit (2 Cor. 13:13; Phil. 2:1, 27). In addition to this, the term also denotes the intimacy that exists between or among those of us who do follow Jesus Christ. In this sense, the essence of biblical fellowship is relational warmth and honesty among believers who are filled with the Spirit and loved by the Son. As Bill Hybels states,

> I know how you're created. You are created to yearn to be in an inner-circle of friends that you trust and that you love, a group of people that you can know and be known by, love and be loved by, serve and be served by, celebrate and be celebrated. So you're all built with the desire to be in those kinds of relationships where you can take the masks off, you can be real and supportive with each other and walk through life closely and do life together. Jesus taught that that's the yearning of everyone's heart.[6]

The two summary passages of Acts 2 and 4 paint for us a remarkable picture of a church that experienced the intimacy of Christian fellowship. In 2:44-45, the first believers "were together and had all things in common; they would sell their possessions and goods and distribute the proceeds to all, as any had need." A similar report appears in 4:32-35, including the phrase, "Now the whole group of those who believed were of one heart and soul...." An intimate church is a church where people take care of each other, a church where a premium is placed on the sharing of people's deepest needs, feelings, and emotions. There is a hunger to know more and to delight in the uniqueness of one another. An intimate church is one that provides a safe place for people to be honest and vulnerable with each other.

It is precisely in this context of fellowship that the work of building relationships happens. This is why the New Testament speaks so often of the importance of *one another*. We are sustained in our journey with God in the fellowship of *one another*. And so we are encouraged to love *one another* (Rom.13:8), honor *one another* (Rom.12:10), be devoted to *one another* (Rom. 12:10), live in harmony with *one another* (Rom. 12:16), accept *one another* (Rom. 15:7), instruct *one another* (Rom. 15:14), agree with *one another* (1 Cor. 1:10), serve *one another* (Gal. 5:13), bear with *one another*

(Eph. 4:2), be kind and compassionate toward *one another* (Eph. 4:32), submit to *one another* (Eph. 5:21), forgive *one another* (Col. 3:13), encourage *one another* (1 Thess. 5:11), live in harmony with *one another* (1 Pet. 3:8), be humble toward *one another* (1 Pet. 5:5), and have fellowship with *one another* (1 John 1:7). You can't miss it. On nearly every page of the New Testament, everything that we are and everything that we do happens in the context of intimate relationships.

Recently, I was preaching one Sunday at a small, rural congregation. Their aged, beloved pastor of many years had recently suffered a stroke and I was called upon to supply the pulpit in his absence. On the several previous Sundays I had been with them, they told me many wonderful stories about their pastor. Every Sunday he was the first person they brought before God during congregational prayer.

My sermon that morning focused on the importance of love in the family of God, and I selected 1 Corinthians 13:4-7 as my text: "Love is patient; love is kind.... It bears all things, believes all things, hopes all things, endures all things." As I slowly made my way through the sermon, I could see how captivated everyone was with this very simple lesson on love. After finishing the sermon, I closed with a brief prayer. The song leader made his way up to the platform to lead us in a final hymn. But before I could make it back to my seat, he intercepted me in the aisle. Gently pulling me to himself, he tearfully embraced me and whispered in my ear, "Reverend Anderson, we really do love each other. It *is* all about love, isn't it?"

I can't remember what the exact title of the closing hymn was that Sunday morning. I do remember well, however, the silent topic that was on the hearts of that congregation. As they sang that final hymn, they all thought of their pastor, themselves, and the love they had for each other in the midst of one of the greatest trials they had ever faced together. That Sunday morning, we shared an intimacy which only God can give and which only believers can experience. The picture of the church we see in the Bible is one of intense fellowship—people with whom we can experience the warmth of intimate and personal relationships in Jesus Christ.

The Church as the Body of Christ

When the New Testament describes the church as the *body of Christ*, it primarily emphasizes the Spirit-endowed giftedness and ministry of the church through which we build up one another. So Paul instructs the believers in Corinth that "when you come together, everyone has a hymn, a lesson, a revelation, a tongue, or an interpretation. Let all things be done for building up" (1 Cor. 14:26). To the Christians in Ephesus he shares similar words:

> But speaking the truth in love, we must grow up in every way into him who is the head, into Christ, from whom the whole body, joined and knit together by every ligament with which it is equipped, as each part is working properly, promotes the body's growth in building itself up in love (4:15-16).

In each of these passages, the central point concerns the connection between spiritual giftedness and the love of people. God does not gift people simply to promote religious busywork, but to assist others in their walk with Christ.

The contemporary rediscovery of spiritual gifts in the church has been refreshing. However, too many so-called *Spiritual Gift Inventories* tend to be little more than psychological profiles which only help people find their *spot* in the church. When the goal of spiritual gift inventories is "spot discovery," too often the practical end result is either death-dealing religious busyness or turf-defending spot wars. "This is *my* spot, and no one is going to take it from me," we might hear someone say. But Paul never had such a thing in mind. Rather, God grants to us the gifts of ministry because he desires for us to plunge into the lives of hurting people. Struggling people often need a personal touch from God, and that touch may very well come through other people like you and me. In describing the church as a body, Paul imagines one member or limb reaching out and assisting another (1 Cor. 12:12; 31).

Stephen Ministry

The great preacher Fred Craddock writes of this when he tells of an occasion early in his ministry:

Before I married and was serving a little mission in the Appalachians, I moved in my service down to a place on Watts Bar Lake between Chattanooga and Knoxville—a little village. It was the custom in that church at Easter to have a baptismal service. My church immerses, and this baptismal service was held in Watts Bar Lake on Easter evening at sundown. Out on a sandbar, I, with the candidates for baptism, moved into the water, and then they moved across to the shore, where the little congregation was gathered singing around the fire and cooking supper. They had constructed little booths for changing clothes, with blankets hanging, and as the candidates moved from the water, they went in and changed clothes and went to the fire in the center. And finally, last of all I went over and changed clothes and went to the fire.

Once we were all around the fire, this is the ritual of that tradition: Glenn Hickey, always Glenn, introduced the new people, gave their names, where they lived, and their work. Then the rest of us formed a circle around them while they stayed warm at the fire. The ritual was each person in the circle gave her or his name and said this:

"My name is Martha, if you ever need somebody to do washing and ironing."

"My name is John, if you ever need anybody to chop wood."

"My name is Emma, if you ever need anybody to babysit."

"My name is Scott, if you ever need anybody to repair your house for you."

"My name is Beverly, if you ever need anybody to sit with the sick."

"My name is Bill, if you ever need a car to go to town."

And around the circle.

Then we ate, and then we had a square dance. And at a time they knew—I didn't know—Percy Miller, with thumbs in his bibbed overalls, would stand up and say, "It's time to go."

Everybody left, and he lingered behind and with his big shoe kicked sand over the dying fire.

At my first experience of that, he saw me standing there still. He looked at me and said, "Craddock, folks don't ever get any closer than this."

In that little community, they have a name for that. I've heard it in other communities, too. In that community, their name for that is 'church'. They call that 'church.'[7]

The picture of the church we see here is that of the body of Christ. As members of that body, God empowers us to reach out and touch others with the gifts of his love.

These, then, are the three pictures of the church that we discover in Scripture. We, the community of faith, are the people of God, an intimate fellowship, and the ministering body of Christ. Just imagine what we can be as we bring these remarkable pictures to life in today's world!

Conclusion

It has been six months now since my family and I arrived at our new church planting assignment. The move has been a hard one, especially in view of our recent resignation and departure from the church we had loved and served for 15 years. Although I have been a Christian for some 25 years, the most exciting 15 years of my journey were those spent at Grace Community Church. I know I was their pastor. Yes, they paid me a salary, occasionally called me "reverend," and even gave me a frozen turkey one Christmas. But I always called the people there "my friends." And what wonderful friends they were. I understand today what it means to belong in a church where people are a priority. I have experienced in simple and practical ways what true intimacy is like in real life. I have witnessed ministry that happened because people were willing to step out of the pew and get involved in the day-to-day struggles of others. Being part of a church like this is a joy that goes beyond words.

As I was driving my two young sons to school this past Monday morning, I noticed they were quieter than usual. After several minutes of hearing nothing but the hum of the heater fan, I reached over to the seat next to me and lightly placed my hand on my 12-year-old son's leg. He continued to stare quietly out the window. After a moment, he turned to me and said, "Dad, I really miss our old church, don't you?" On hearing this from the back seat, my eight-year-old boy eagerly unhooked his seat belt, scooted forward and joined in the conversation. "Me too, Dad, I miss it too. It was so fun there!" he said. And so we traveled down the road, talking and laughing together in these delightful remembrances of Grace Community Church. Soon we arrived in the parking lot at the school. We said a quick prayer together as we waited in line for the drop off. Then, I let them out and began my drive to the office. And as I drove, I thought to myself, "What wonderful, beautiful memories my children have of church. I'm really a lucky dad!" And I prayed, "Thank you God—thank you for my kids. Thank you for your faithfulness. And above all, thank you for this thing called 'church.'"

Discussion Questions

1. *Evangelism and Community*: What are the consequences and dangers of a church that seeks to be evangelistic but neglects to foster meaningful community? Can a church be truly evangelistic without emphasizing community? Can a church be a true community without being genuinely evangelistic?

2. *Church Size and Community*: Do you feel that church size affects the development of community? Is there a size beyond which a church can no longer maintain and nurture the core value of community? Are smaller churches necessarily better suited to the tasks discussed in this chapter (people, fellowship, and body)? Or do larger churches actually hold some advantages over smaller churches with respect to building intimacy and community?

3. *The Pastor and Community*: Is it a good thing for the preacher of the church to be someone *other than* the pastor of the church?

Should the preaching pastor of a congregation be intimately aware and involved in the needs and circumstances of the people to whom he or she preaches? Are there any examples in the New Testament where the leader of a church was not personally involved in the details and lives of those following?

4. *Expansion and Community*: It has been said that "values come and go." What are the prospects that we in the Brethren in Christ Church will maintain our commitment to community as we grow, diversify, and expand as a denomination? Are the prospects favorable or unfavorable? How will we as a church know when we have compromised our commitment to community? What can we as a denomination do year by year to cultivate and develop that commitment?

5. *Denominational Community*: A sense of community at the local church level is an easy concept to comprehend. But is a sense of community possible at the denominational level? How does our core value of community affect our life together at the level of regional and general church affairs? Do the principles of community apply here? Should the principles of community apply here?

6. *Diversity and Community*: How do we build community out of diversity? And how do concerns of gender, race, and economic standing affect our commitment to the building of Christian community? Are we building communities where everyone is truly welcome and indeed welcomed into *all* aspects of our life and ministries? Or are there places in our life together where some are allowed and others excluded?

7. *Technology and Community*: How can we utilize technology in building community? Is the internet a friend or foe of our core value? Does the personal computer alienate or unite in terms of personal relationships with people? Can a sense of community be achieved outside of proximate, personal contact with others?

8. In what ways can church programs and church "things" take priority and precedence over the care and value of people? How can this be avoided?

9. A difficult problem arises within the life of your local church. People hold differing opinions on the matter and soon begin to take sides on the issue. Both sides feel they are right. Both sides believe that their own position should prevail. What are the qualities and values of Brethren in Christ people which would prove helpful in bringing a successful, redemptive resolution to this scenario? What would our liabilities be? Does the Brethren in Christ Church have a better "track record" than other groups when it comes to conflict resolution? Why or why not?

10. In what ways is God encouraging you to grow relationally closer with other Christians? What are the things that may cause you to resist this calling?

For Further Reading

Bilezikian, Gilbert. *Community 101: Reclaiming the Church as Community of Oneness.* Grand Rapids, Mich.: Zondervan Publishing House, 1993.

Bonhoeffer, Dietrich. *Life Together.* Reprint ed. San Francisco: Harper and Row, 1978.

Crabb, Larry. *Connecting.* Nashville: Word Publishing, 1997.

Snyder, Howard. *Community of the King.* Downers Grove, Il.: InterVarsity Press, 1978.

Vanier, Jean. *Community and Growth.* Mahwah, N.J.: Paulist Press, 1989.

6

Witnessing to the World

We value an active and loving witness for Christ to all people.

by Craig E. Sider

*There's nothing like the adventure of being
used by God to contagiously spread His love, truth, and
life to other people—people who deeply matter to him.*[1]
—*Bill Hybels and Mark Mittelberg*

Entering into a new relationship with God through salvation is an awesome experience. The Brethren in Christ firmly believe that this wonderful relationship is designed for every person on the planet— bar none. Every person created has a vacuum longing to be filled through a discovery of God's love and grace.

As a little boy in Sunday school, I sang a simple song that captures and declares God's love for the world:

> Jesus loves the little children,
> all the children of the world.
> Red and yellow, black and white,
> they are precious in his sight,
> Jesus loves the little children of the world.

This song expresses well a value that is at the heart of our church—a desire to see others experience the love and grace of God.

To hoard this gift, contain this gift, or even delight in such a gift to the exclusion of others, is unthinkable. The heart of God is a giving, outward-focused heart. Therefore, "we value an active and loving witness for Christ to all people."

Witnessing is a God Thing

Christians who witness to the work of God in their lives reflect the heart of God. The Bible introduces a Creator God who reaches out to his creation to bring them back into relationship with him. God is always reaching out. Early in the biblical landscape, he sends Abraham out from his own land and family, promising to bless all the peoples of the world through him if he obeys (Gen. 12:1-3). Later, God sends Joseph into Egypt in order to preserve Abraham's descendants during a time of famine (Gen. 45:4-8). God sends Moses to this people, now called Israelites, in order to lead them out of slavery in Egypt to the Promised Land (Exod. 3:10). Over the centuries that followed, God used prophets to bring both words of warning and promise to his people. So we have glimpses, all through the Old Testament, of God's desire to bring salvation to the nations. Through the prophet Isaiah, he declares to his people, "I will also make you a light for the Gentiles, that you may bring my salvation to the ends of the earth" (Isa. 49:6).

At just the right time, God sent his Son, Jesus, as this light to the world (Isa. 49:6; Luke 2:32). Jesus was the light to which the prophets pointed. Jesus was the Lamb of God destined to take away the sin of the world. Throughout his life on earth, Jesus went to spiritually disenfranchised people, proclaiming a message of hope and forgiveness. In Luke 15 he tells three stories—about a lost sheep, lost coin, and lost son—in response to Pharisaical mutterings over his "going" to the lost sinners of the day. Jesus continued the sending motif that begins back in the book of Genesis. After Jesus' crucifixion and resurrection, God the Father sealed the work of the Son by sending his Spirit on the Day of Pentecost. Truly, God is a sending God.

And Jesus clearly intended for this sending to be multiplied in his followers. As an extension of his preaching, teaching, and healing ministry, he sent out the twelve apostles and, later, seventy-two disciples (Luke 10). In John 17, Jesus declares that he sends out his followers just as the Father has sent him out. After his resurrection, Jesus gives a clear call to his followers to go and make disciples of all nations as they witness in the power of the Holy Spirit (Matt. 28:19; Acts 1:8). Jesus' call to his disciples to "go" is certainly not restricted to those who heard him that day. It is a call to everyone, throughout all time, who declares allegiance to his kingdom.

Everyone who has experienced God's grace is now charged to continue the "sending motif" of God. Every believer is called to be a witness as God sustains his redemption plan for the world. And so the sending continues.

Motivation for Witness

To be "an active and loving witness for Christ" encompasses one's entire life, as our words, actions, and lifestyle all give off a fragrant aroma of God's love and grace. The hope is that those outside the family of God will be drawn by this fragrance to repent of their sin, trust Jesus Christ for the forgiveness of sin, and follow Christ in wholehearted obedience. What is that internal compass in a believer that is always pointing toward a life of witness?

Full Awareness of Our Spiritual Wealth

A friend, Marlene, spoke to me with tears in her eyes. "I can't believe how good God has been to me. To know how much God loves me is incredible!" She continued for ten minutes telling of God's faithfulness and transforming power in her life. "We have an incredible God," she said. As I listened, it was so obvious that she wasn't about to keep this wealth to herself.

This is not a new phenomenon. The ninth chapter of John tells the story of a blind man whose life had been spent with his hands outstretched—until he encountered Christ. Jesus healed this blind beggar and stirred up a hornets' nest of controversy. This man's life was so transformed that some questioned whether he was the same man who had begged since birth. The religious leaders of the day questioned Jesus' credentials because the healing took place on the Sabbath. The Pharisees peppered this healed man with questions, finally asking "What do you say about him?" His response was clear and simple: "One thing I do know, that though I was blind, now I see" (v. 25).

Witnessing isn't a burdensome task to be performed. It is the natural response of an overflowing heart. Marlene couldn't help herself. She had to tell me about her new life in Christ. The newly-sighted beggar in John 9 was spontaneously expressing the joy of his life. When believers live with a fresh awareness of how rich they are—the extent of their inheritance in Christ, the wonder of the God they worship, the miracle of new birth and a transformed life—they are compelled to be witnesses for the Savior.

Believers conscious of their God-wealth find themselves saying to lost people, "You just need to know how wonderful our God is." A primary motivation in being a witness for Christ is a joy-filled awareness of one's spiritual blessings. Something so rich and so good begs to be shared.

Counts for Eternity

At the same time, believers know what it means for someone to live and die apart from Christ. Christ is more than a "nice thing" for people to have. Knowing Christ is absolutely necessary.

Jesus wept over the city of Jerusalem. He had compassion on the crowds because of their separation from the shepherd. The stories he told in Luke 15 about the lost sheep, the lost coin, and the lost son point to the raw truth that people are lost, needing to be found. Likewise, the letters of the apostle Paul are filled with his awareness of what is eternally at stake for people. People who have not received new life in Christ are spiritually separated from God. If they die in that state, they will experience separation from God for eternity in a place called hell.

When believers are gripped by the fact that nice people, including their neighbors and friends, are on a road that leads to destruction, their mindset is forever affected. They think, "She's not just a lawyer; she's someone for whom Christ died. My neighbors are not just a banker, a teller, a waitress, a broker, a teacher; they are people for whom Christ died." God has gone to great lengths to rescue them from an eternity apart from him. That's the bare truth. As Christians view people as individuals who need Christ in order to experience fullness of life on this earth and for eternity, their motivation gains a keen sense of urgency and definiteness.

Where Am I to Witness?

The direction of movement in Acts 1:8 is outward. Jesus tells his disciples that their ministry will begin from where they are and then move outward in concentric circles, first to neighboring Judea, then to Samaria, and from there to the ends of the earth. Witnessing begins where we stand.

There is a built-in strength to this approach. God has placed us in a location from which we are to begin our witnessing endeavors. The town where I live, Elizabethtown, is my "Jerusalem." I begin my witnessing endeavors in this community; to the neighbors next to my home, to the teller at my bank, to the cashier at the corner mini-market. These people—Charlie, Doug, Matt, and Tracy—are my immediate mission field. Witnessing is up-close and personal and begins where God has placed me.

Yet we must be very careful. As people, we tend to gravitate toward what is familiar and easily identifiable. The people we interact with and the country where we reside are, from our view-point, the "center" of the world. We tend to look at God's plan of redemption from that perspective. We must be aware that the place where we live is only one part of the world for which Christ died. God loves people in all those other dots on the globe just as he loves people in the dot you and I happen to inhabit. Jesus offered his life and blood for the sins of the Iranian, the Slav, the Hispanic, and the Chinese, just as he did for you and me.[2]

Further, the challenge of telling the whole world the good news of Jesus is complicated by the distribution of those who have already heard. Christians are not evenly spread across the globe. At some places, many miles and cultural barriers separate the millions who walk with Christ from the millions who have never heard the name of Jesus. We need to be reminded that God deeply loves these least-reached people and that he died for them as much as he died for you and me. How significant are the words of the apostle Paul: "…how are they to hear without someone to proclaim him (Jesus)? And how are they to proclaim him unless they are sent? As it is written, 'How beautiful are the feet of those who bring good news!'" (Rom. 10:14-15).

To sum up, witnessing started at Jerusalem, but was never designed to stay there. The witness of the first disciples was to move increasingly outward, widening as it spread. The same is true for believers today. Witnessing begins at home, but moves continually outward to all nations.

What Do We Want to Accomplish?

What is the purpose behind building an authentic relationship with a nonbelieving neighbor? Why does someone from Kansas leave family and home and travel to Singapore in order to declare the message of Christ? Why does a Korean believer leave the comforts and familiarity of Seoul and locate in Los Angeles to be near "her people"? Why does a grandparent engage in ceaseless prayer for a wayward grandson? What motivates a salesman striving to be an effective witness on the job? In 1 Timothy 2:3-4, the apostle Paul answers: "God…desires everyone to be saved and to come to the knowledge of the truth."

We witness to the saving grace of Christ in our lives with the hope that men, women, boys and girls will come to a living knowledge of the truth. We desire to expand the kingdom of God and deplete the kingdom of darkness. We long for those held captive by Satan to be released. With hearts that echo the heart of God, we want all people to be saved and come to know Christ.

For this reason, we don't want our witnessing efforts to translate into short-lived decisions for Christ. Our goal in witnessing is the transformation of a life. Warren Hoffman, a leader in the Brethren in Christ Church, states it this way in his book *The Secret of the Harvest*:

> Our goal...is not simply to invite persons to make the decision to establish or re-establish a personal relationship with Christ, although this is of absolute importance. Rather, it is to help them to establish basic Christian commitments and lifestyle patterns that will be fruitful for years to come.[3]

Jesus anticipates "fruit that will last" (John 13:35). Our aim in witnessing is to help people to make decisions that will impact them for a lifetime. This motivation brings precision and focus to our witnessing endeavors.

Our witnessing, therefore, must be more than a call to "hang your hat" at church. George Gallup Jr. indicates that this practice of church attendance appears to make little difference in people's ethical views and behavior with respect to lying, cheating, pilferage, and not reporting theft.[4] Our witness needs to point to the need to repent of one's sin before a holy God, to receive the free gifts of salvation available through the work of Christ, and also to allow the Lord to transform one's life into his likeness. The heart of our witness, both through lifestyle and through words, is a call to allow Christ to transform life.

Believers Respond!

Who's going to win the world for Christ? It is tempting to think that the world will be won for Christ by gifted evangelists that, we may think, are surely the ones God has designed to make the biggest splash in impacting lost people. We see ourselves as mere background players who might pray and give, but leading people to Christ is beyond us.

Whenever I encounter the temptation to think this way, one of my treasured memories comes to mind. It was one hour before I was to leave for Pennsylvania to assume the responsibilities of a bishop in the church. It was my final hour as pastor of Upper Oaks Church in Oakville, Ontario. Seventy people were standing around a backyard swimming pool in which three people were to be baptized as a declaration of their faith in Christ. Before friends and family, Dana declared his faith in Jesus, and he thanked the body of Christ at Upper Oaks for their acceptance of him and for their gentle witness. As I listened, I knew it wasn't the effort of one dynamic individual that impacted Dana most significantly. Rather, it was the consistent witness of many who allowed the "music of Christ" to play through their lives.

Every believer, without exception, is given the witness mandate. In Matthew 28:18-20 Jesus announces the commission, "Go therefore and make disciples of all nations, baptizing them in the name of the Father and of the Son and of the Holy Spirit, and teaching them to obey everything that I have commanded you." Just before his ascension to heaven, Jesus met with his apostles and declared, "you will receive power when the Holy Spirit has come upon you, and you will be my witness...." (Acts 1:8).

The apostle Paul carries this commission to the enlarging church as he charges the Philippian Christians to live like Christ so that they may "shine like stars in the world" (Phil. 2:15). He similarly encourages Philemon to be active in sharing his faith (Philemon vs. 6). Writing to Christians scattered by persecution, the apostle Peter encourages them to "always be ready to make your defense to anyone who demands from you an accounting for the hope that is in you; yet do it with gentleness and reverence" (1 Pet. 3:15). At no place in the Bible is witnessing limited to an "elite" squad.

Scripture is clear that the task of witnessing is for every believer, not just a chosen few. The church understood this from the beginning. The chief agents in the expansion of Christianity in the early church were the masses. It was not

> those who made it a profession or made it a major part of their occupation, but men and women who carried on their livelihood in some purely secular manner and spoke of their faith to those they met in this natural fashion.[5]

Throughout the last 2000 years, believers, witnessing in relative obscurity, have continued the spread of the gospel. And so it is today. Every Christian is called and needed in the witnessing arena.

A Believer in Action

How then, with our diversity of gifts, personalities and abilities, do we let an unbelieving world know of the Good News of Jesus Christ? How do we shine the light of our witness close at home and also extend its brilliance around the world?

Witness Begins with Prayer

Once a week for ten years, Steve and I met with a changing lineup of six or so men in the offices of Upper Oaks. Our purpose was simple; we gathered to pray. On a whiteboard we wrote the names of folks that we were praying for to come to faith in Christ. In almost every case, the names that went on the board were persons with a connection to at least one of us. After listing the names, we would pray. We prayed that God, through his Spirit, would work in their lives, drawing them to himself. We prayed for our sensitivity and courage in being effective witnesses. Most pointedly, we prayed that each individual would come to the point of decision to trust and follow Jesus Christ. And an amazing thing happened: over that ten-year span, dozens of those individuals came to trust Christ. God "just happened" to use us in their faith discovery.

Prayer—pure and simple—is the starting point for effective witness. Our partnership with God in making him known begins on our knees. In the mystery of God's economy, our prayer prompts God to speak to people through his Spirit. The Holy Spirit stirs a spiritual awakening and brings people to an awareness of their sin.

Praying also has a profound effect on those of us who pray. As we pray for people's spiritual needs, the Holy Spirit prompts us to caring action. God gives us insight to communicate his truth with spiritual power and with sensitivity. Praying for others' salvation motivates us, energizes us, and gives us courage to reach out to others in witness. Prayer is the starting point for witness.

Individuals who consistently and specifically pray for others to come to faith in Christ are agents in the conversion of men and women. Imagine what would happen if we engaged in some of the following prayer activities!

- praying daily for three people to come to faith in Christ
- walking regularly through our neighborhoods and praying for the folks living in each house
- gathering with a group of men, women, or youth and praying for the salvation of specific individuals
- praying each morning that God's Spirit would give us sensitivity to witnessing prompts throughout the day
- asking God to empower us to live a holy life each day
- praying that God would raise up men and women to declare the message of Christ to unheard people groups
- praying for courage, empowerment, and clarity in witnessing

The truth of the matter is, prayer changes things. Prayer unleashes the activity of God in others and in us. Prayer is the starting point for a life of witness.

Witness "In the World"

For our witness to be effective we need to be "in the world." This involves rubbing shoulders and building relationships with those outside the family of God. We then come to know them by name. We learn to know their families, their heartaches and desires. Even though we are members of a different kingdom, we penetrate their world.

Jesus proclaimed his followers to be the salt of the earth and the light of the world (Matt. 5:13-16). Both of these analogies presume contact for effectiveness. Salt, as Rebecca Pippert has so aptly reminded us, only has effect outside of the salt shaker.[6] Likewise, light is an illuminating reality only in the midst of darkness. Jesus said it about as clearly as it can be stated:

> A city built on a hill cannot be hid. No one after lighting a lamp puts it under the bushel basket, but on the lampstand,

> and it gives light to all in the house. In the same way, let your
> light shine before others, so that they may see your good works
> and give glory to your Father in heaven (Matt. 5:14-16).

And Jesus modeled this close proximity. As you scan through the pages of the Gospels, you consistently find him rubbing shoulders with irreligious people. You find him at a well with a Samaritan woman (John 4), at a party with Matthew's irreligious colleagues (Luke 5:29), with tax collectors and sinners (Luke 15), and eating dinner with a despised publican named Zacchaeus (Luke 19). Jesus displayed incarnational witnessing in both his birth and in his life and ministry.

This sounds easy, but it takes a determined spirit. Often our identity in the family of God results in us forming relationships exclusively within the church. We are most comfortable with those who share our values. At worst, we "circle the wagons" to keep others out and to keep ourselves pure. Left to our own inclinations, we have a tendency to withdraw. Leighton Ford makes this observation:

> Many Christians have been so afraid of being contaminated by
> worldliness that they have avoided any social contacts with
> unconverted persons. As a result, they have no natural bridge
> for evangelism; what witnessing they do is usually artificial and
> forced rather than the spontaneous outgrowth of genuine
> friendship.[7]

Christians who intentionally build relationships with folks outside the kingdom position themselves for a lifetime of witness. We may impress people from a distance, but we can only impact them up close.

Witnessing "in the world" has its greatest impact when two things are true. First, we must be known for having a distinctive presence. Followers of Christ are true light and true salt to the extent that a holy distinction pervades their lifestyle. From the grand sweep of life to the minutest detail, Christians walk to the beat of a different drummer. To forgive seventy times seven (Matt. 18:22), pray for those who persecute us (Matt. 5:44), resist the urge to store up "treasures on earth" (Matt. 6:19-20), love our neighbor as ourselves (Mark 12:31), remember the poor (Gal. 2:10), and live "holy and godly lives" (2 Peter 3:11) is to display a beauty of life that points to the God we serve.

Second, our close proximity has its greatest impact when we look at people through the eyes of Jesus—past the facades and exteriors and to the issues of the heart. When we see the agonies and the sorrows that people experience, we become God's agents to those desperately in need of love. More than feeling sorry, we reach out and touch. In the truest sense, we display God's character—his love, his righteousness, his justice, and his faithfulness—through the particulars of our everyday lives.[8] We are salt and light. We make a difference because, in Christ, we are different.

Witnessing is Telling the Story

Our witness begins with "presence" and proceeds to proclamation. These two are twins. In his very helpful book, *Evangelism in the Early Church*, Michael Green states: "Christianity is enshrined in the life: but it is proclaimed by the lips. If there is a failure in either respect the gospel cannot be communicated."[9] Joe Aldrich writes even more graphically, "...presence which never leads to proclamation is an extreme to be avoided. We are 'fishers of men,' sent to catch fish, not frogmen who dive under water and swim with the fish, making our 'presence' known."[10]

God has gifted some of his children to be bold proclaimers of the gospel. The apostle Paul epitomizes the kind of person who walks into an area, sizes up the crowd, and boldly proclaims the good news of Christ. Today, when individuals are gifted in this way, we need to "fan the flame" so that their bold proclamation can be used to advance the kingdom.

However, most of us are not wired this way. By nature, we are not as verbal, as assertive, or as direct. We may not think on our feet as gifted apologists do. Sadly, we make the erroneous assumption that our witness is to be only one of presence, not of proclamation. We decide to leave proclamation to the talkers.

To be sure, bold proclaimers of the gospel are important in witness. But individuals gifted in evangelism will win only a small percentage of the people in this world to Christ. To relegate all proclamation to a few extroverted and dynamic Christians is to sell short the activity of God's Spirit in the life of every believer. In his book *Honest to God*, Bill Hybels declares God's intention to use every believer in the proclamation of the gospel:

> The unbelieving world is made up of a variety of people; young and old, rich and poor, educated and uneducated, urban and rural, with different races, personalities, values, political systems, and religious backgrounds. Isn't it obvious it would take more than one style of evangelist to reach such a diverse population.... Somewhere in that multifarious group is a person who needs an evangelist of your exact age, career, and level of spiritual understanding, or of my exact personality, background, and interests.[11]

As Christians pray for others within their sphere of influence to find Christ, as they display a beauty of life that reflects Christ, as they live in the world and respond to needs in the way of Christ, they will find themselves being asked about Christ. The apostle Peter charges us to "always be ready to make your defense to anyone who demands from you an accounting for the hope that is in you" (1 Peter 3:15).

What makes proclamation by every believer so powerful is that the story of Christ is communicated through a life that has been touched by his love. No one has a faith story quite like mine or quite like yours. And as each believer sharpens the ability to tell their story and to share the salvation story, the opportunities for kingdom advancement are dramatically increased.

The Church in Action

In addition to witnessing for Christ as individuals, the larger body of believers carries out various functions that contribute to the spreading of the gospel throughout the world.

The Local Church

God's strategy for redeeming the world involves a beautiful bride. In the New Testament, the Church is called the "Bride of Christ" (2 Cor. 11:2; Eph. 5:21-33; Rev. 19:7). The apostle Paul explains that Christ loved and gave himself for the church so that she might be presented "holy and without blemish" (Eph. 5:27). The beauty of the bride of Christ—the church—is a powerful component in a loving and active witness to the world.

A powerful dynamic can occur when believers come together in a local church. A local church that mirrors the qualities of Christ displays divine signposts for an unbelieving world. These divine signposts are able to draw and point individuals to a loving and gracious God.[12] Simply put, the church being the church is a significant component of witness.

When the church is a caring community, nonbelievers are attracted by the dynamic of loving relationships. In an atmosphere of caring concern, the truth is spoken in love. An attitude of acceptance prevails. When one person suffers, the body suffers with that person. When one person rejoices, the body joins in the celebration. In a church like this, admonitions to forgive one another, to encourage one another, to comfort one another, and to bear one another's burdens are taken seriously. Jesus said, "everyone will know that you are my disciples, if you have love for one another" (John 13:35).

Unity is also a powerful signpost to an unbelieving world. In his prayer recorded in John 17, Jesus prays that all future believers will be brought to complete unity *to let the world know* that God sent him and has loved them (italics mine). When nonbelievers, looking on, see church fights, schisms, gossip, manipulation, and politicking, they say, "they're no different than we are." However, when a diverse group of believers comes together in a local church, refuses to give in to destructive patterns of disunity, and instead, is characterized by unity and harmony, a nonbelieving world says, "this must be of God."

Another distinctive signpost of the church is good works. Few would deny that a dominant drive in our society is to seek convenience, cater to personal desires and affirm self interest. In the midst of this me-centered world, a church noted for good works displays a compelling signpost for nonbelievers. In Ephesians 2:10 we are told that "we are what he (God) has made us, created in Christ Jesus for good works." A church that feeds the hungry, clothes the naked, ministers to the widow and the orphan, and cares for the poor and disenfranchised is an active and loving witness to Christ. Whether such action involves building a school in Honduras, serving at an inner-city soup kitchen or development program, or building a home through Habitat for Humanity, it is a powerful and appealing contrast to the prevailing self-centered orientation of the culture.

Finally, hope is a divine signpost of the church to a world caught in the clutches of despair. Believers and nonbelievers alike experience tragedies, sorrows, and pain. Christians are not immune to the difficulties of life. Yet we do not "grieve as others do who have no hope" (1 Thess. 4:13). While the church recognizes pain and suffering and hurts with those who hurt, it is a bastion of hope. Believers know that the best is yet to come. They are hope-filled people. They know that nothing can take away the inheritance that belongs to those in the body of Christ. This living hope impacts the church's view of eternity, and it also ushers in a freedom to live boldly and courageously in the present age. This anticipation and confidence of the church is salt and light to an often hopeless world.

Church Planting

Starting new churches is the most effective way to reach people outside the kingdom. Studies consistently show that conversions to Christ happen with greater frequency in newer congregations. One outstanding witness opportunity for a church or a cluster of churches is to reproduce themselves by launching new churches. By adopting a multiplication mindset, a local church expands its witness and models the sending motif of our giving God.

Starting new churches is not a new trend. The apostle Paul engaged in this kingdom-expanding activity as he traveled from city to city proclaiming the gospel. Paul knew that as the church was established in an ever-increasing number of towns and cities, opportunities increased for nonbelievers to discover new life in Christ. New churches resulted in conversions. They still do today.

Christian Schwarz performed an exhaustive study of one thousand churches in 32 countries from five continents. He studied large and small churches across a broad spectrum of cultures and theological perspectives to discover the key components of a healthy church. As he looked at churches across the world, he concluded:

> Hardly anything demonstrates the health of a congregation as much as the willingness—and ability!—to give birth to new congregations. The opposite is true as well. Hardly anything is a more clear indication of illness than structures which by design hinder church multiplication, or at best permit it as an absolute exception.[13]

We need a renewed vision for church planting that will prompt local churches, either singly or in clusters, to start healthy and reproducing "daughter" churches. These initiatives need not be limited to large churches. Congregations of any size can be directly involved in daughtering a new congregation. They can commit to be a prayer team, provide financial support, and send families to be part of the new group. I am convinced that God blesses churches that actively engage in church multiplication in special ways.

World Missions

The best known verse in Scripture begins, "For God so loved the world…" (John 3:16). Jesus was sent as a light to the world. Following his resurrection, Christ gave his disciples the scope of their mission: "make disciples of all nations." That mandate threads its way through time and, without losing one bit of strength, calls the church today to the same breadth of task.

The dawn of a new millennium is a good time to reflect on what has happened over the world in the past century.[14] In 1900:

- only 8 percent of the world's languages had any portion of Scripture
- about 0.4 percent of the total population of Latin America, Africa and Asia could have been considered evangelical Christians
- only 8,000-9,000 missionaries were focused on the people of these lands

After two world wars, a wave of passion to reach the world for Christ turned into a flood. Missionary endeavors multiplied as many church groups, including the Brethren in Christ, recommitted themselves to world evangelization. Today evangelicals worldwide are growing three times faster than the population. During the past 100 years, over 50 percent of the population of the African continent was radically affected by new life in Christ. Evangelicals in Latin America increased from under 250,000 to around 40 million in the same period. Today there are more evangelicals in Asia then in North America. Of the ten largest evangelical congregations in the world, seven are in Seoul, Korea, where no church existed 110 years ago!

Although great progress is occurring, the task is far from finished. About 2 billion individuals in our world still live in ethno-linguistic groups where few if any churches exist. The task of the church is to reach each person of every successive generation with the transforming person of Christ—to take the gospel to every person. This happens best when attempted by a church with a similar cultural/ language context as the unevangelized. Thus, the church, once established within a people group, carries responsibility to spread the good news within the same cultural/language group.

Individual believers and churches alike are called to God's vision for the whole world. With nearly 1600 large groups of people still waiting for the development of viable churches in their midst, the opportunities are great! Men and women of passion who are skillfully trained and sent out to minister to unreached people groups are needed. Local congregations who will commit themselves to a ministry of prayer and to unselfish giving for those who are sent are needed as well. As we focus on God's ultimate desire for the peoples of the earth, we will see the fulfillment of God's plan when representatives from every group of people on planet earth gather before the throne to worship Jesus.

Conclusion

As followers of Jesus, we are people of privilege. We have experienced forgiveness of sins, adoption into God's family, the joy of his presence, fellowship in his body, a life of fulfillment, the promise of heaven, and much more. That we should be recipients of such incredibly great gifts is a tribute to God's abundant grace and mercy. From such a privileged position we have been given another privilege, the privilege of witness. We have the delight of being God's agents in demonstrating and declaring his love to the world. And so we heartily sing:

> This little light of mine, I'm gonna let it shine,
> This little light of mine, I'm gonna let it shine,
> Let it shine, let it shine, let it shine.
>
> Let it shine 'til Jesus comes, I'm gonna let it shine,
> Let it shine 'til Jesus comes, I'm gonna let it shine,
> Let it shine, let it shine, let it shine.

Discussion Questions

1. Do you view witnessing more as a burden or privilege? What actions can believers take to be fully aware of their wealth in Christ?

2. Are people really eternally lost apart from Christ? Is this truth a deeply held value among those in your church? What place should the reality of hell have in witnessing endeavors?

3. Is it possible to be nearsighted with respect to witnessing and ignore the rest of the world? Is it possible to be farsighted and neglect your lost coworker or neighbor? What corrective measures can be taken?

4. Jesus said he anticipates fruit that will last (John 13:35). Can the gospel be presented in such a way that people's decisions for Christ are short-lived? How much of the Christian message must be incorporated into witnessing endeavors for persons to truly understand salvation?

5. The author suggests that praying for people (to come to Christ) impacts both them and us. Explore the impact of prayer on the lost and on those who witness. What steps can individuals and groups of believers take to develop a consistent evangelistic prayer ministry?

6. Leighton Ford observes that Christians have a tendency to withdraw to themselves in relationships. What are your comfort zones and what would it take for you to venture out of them? What would motivate you to venture into others' comfort zones? How can you most meaningfully connect with irreligious people?

7. What kind of behavior from today's Christians will intrigue non-Christians enough to cause them to investigate faith in Christ? How would your non-Christian friends respond to the question "what good news does the church have for the world?"

8. How would you share the meaning of salvation without using religious words?

9. The statement has been made that "starting new churches is the most effective way to reach people outside the kingdom." Why do you think this is the case? How can you and your church be actively involved in church planting? What 'threat factors' need to be overcome in daughtering a church?

10. Are you encouraged or discouraged when you think of world evangelization? How can your church make a difference in taking the gospel to unreached people groups? Is it appropriate to say "we're not really a world missions church"? Why or why not?

For Further Reading

Green, Michael. *Evangelism in the Early Church.* Grand Rapids, Mich.: Eerdmans Publishing Company, 1970.

Hoffman, Warren. *Secret of the Harvest.* Nappanee, Ind.: Evangel Press, 1988.

Hybels, Bill, and Mark Mittelberg. *Becoming a Contagious Christian.* Grand Rapids, Mich.: Zondervan Publishing Company, 1994.

Posterski, Donald C. *Reinventing Evangelism: New Strategies for Presenting Christ in Today's World.* Downers Grove, Ill.: Inter-Varsity Press, 1989.

Sweet, Leonard. *Aqua Church: Essential Leadership Arts for Piloting Your Church in Today's Fluid Culture.* Loveland, Co.: Group, 1999.

7

Serving Compassionately

*We value serving others at their point of need,
following the example of our Lord Jesus.*

by Paul Lehman-Schletewitz

*For the Son of Man came not to be served but to serve,
and to give his life a ransom for many.*
—Jesus Christ (Mark 10:45)

Our excursion to Disneyland was one of the last trips I took with my parents before moving away to college. Through a series of tradeoffs, we enjoyed a wonderful time together. I sat through the Enchanted Tikki Room, and Dad rode the Matterhorn with me. But it was now the end of a very long day, and my father was driving us home. Startled, I awoke from a sound sleep when the car suddenly stopped, and Dad threw open his door and jumped out.

Generally speaking, my father never stopped during a trip. But on this occasion, another car had turned left into oncoming traffic. By the time we got to the accident, some of the bystanders had already pulled the injured couple from the wreckage. The men in the offending vehicle had abandoned their disabled auto and fled into the night. At the scene, both the reflection of the street lamp on the shiny wet asphalt and the smell of gasoline around the couple's crumpled car signaled immediate danger.

The young husband lay still and moaned deeply, while his wife cried hysterically. Both were severely injured. My father took off his coat and covered the bleeding man. He then asked me for my sweater, which he used to pillow the woman's head. The panic in the air was palpable, and it worsened with each scream from the bleeding woman. Dad asked, "Has anyone called for help?," Fortunately, someone had. Quietly, my Mom and Dad bent over the hurting couple and began to pray with them. Soon, the screaming stopped and a sense of peace and reassurance settled on the scene. In the distance the sound of an ambulance could be heard, but help had already arrived.

I left the scene of the accident that night without my sweater, but I took with me a changed heart. By stopping to help those in need, my Dad demonstrated for me the power of serving others for Christ. I learned forever that a few simple acts of sacrificial service can change both a situation as well as the people involved.[1]

Service in The Bible

In the opening chapter of Genesis, God created the world and declared it "good" (Gen. 1:10-31). This creation was characterized in every respect by perfect harmony. God, people, and nature worked together for the betterment of all. Even the call to exercise dominion over the rest of creation gave human beings the responsibility, not to fend solely for themselves, but to care for all that God made.[2]

Such harmony, however, disappeared when humanity chose to disobey God. By seeking equality with God (Gen. 3:5), people abandoned service in favor of self-advancement.[3] Soon, all of creation suffered the terrible consequences (3:14-24). Since then, God's plan of redemption has sought to restore the rightful place of service in the hearts and minds of otherwise self-centered human beings.

In the Old Testament, God's efforts to encourage service took the form of both reminders and laws. With respect to reminders, the people of Israel were frequently told that they themselves had been slaves in Egypt before God miraculously brought them out. Therefore, they should likewise assist others who experience various types of needs (e.g., Lev. 19:34; Deut. 24:17-18, 21). In terms of laws, specific commandments appear within Israel's legal codes that instruct the people to serve those in difficulty. For example, farmers were required to leave grain and produce in their fields and vineyards so that the poor could find food (Lev. 19:9-10; Deut. 24: 19-21). From the start, God elevated service to others as a vital characteristic of his people.

It is perhaps in the mission of the anticipated Messiah, however, that this call to service finds its clearest expression. This mission, outlined so vividly in Isaiah's description of the suffering servant (Isa. 42, 49, 50, and 53), exposes the manner in which redemption will come to the creation. According to Isaiah, the servant will perform his task in quiet gentleness (42:2-3) and with great persistence (42:4). Through the service of this same messianic servant, though he will be hated and despised (49:7; 50:6-7; 53:3-5), God will shine his light of salvation throughout the world (53:4-5; 11-12):

> Surely he has borne our infirmities
>   and carried our diseases;
> yet we accounted him stricken,
>   struck down by God, and afflicted.
> But he was wounded for our
>   transgressions,
>   crushed for our iniquities;
> upon him was the punishment
>   that made us whole,
>   and by his bruises we are healed.
>
> (Isaiah 53:4-5)

In short, the servant will serve others without limit, doing for them what they are incapable of doing for themselves.

In painting a picture of how God's redemptive plan will be accomplished, these ancient songs of service lead into the New Testament by providing the backdrop to the ministry of Jesus. Jesus, the suffering servant anticipated by Isaiah, "did not come to be served but to serve, and to give his life a ransom for many" (Mark 10:45). In these few words, Jesus summed up both his mission and the means by which he would accomplish it. His goal is the ransom of many. His means is through sacrificial service. He touched "untouchable" lepers, raised the "unraiseable" cripple, and healed the "unhealable" blind (Mark 1:40; 2:1-12; 8:22-26). Yet his death on the cross, anticipated in Isaiah 53, presents the highest expression of Jesus' servant ministry. As the apostle Paul writes,

> Let the same mind be in you that was in Christ Jesus,
> who, though he was in the form
> of God,
> did not regard equality with
> God
> as something to be exploited,
> but emptied himself,
> taking the form of a slave,
> being born in human likeness.
> and being found in human form,
> he humbled himself
> and became obedient to the
> point of death—
> even death on a cross.

(Phil. 2:5-8)

Jesus, through his servant ministry, perfectly fulfilled his divine task. In his life, death and resurrection, Jesus modeled service to every human need. Rather than exclusively "saving people's souls" and transporting them to eternal bliss, he continued his Father's plan and reached out to all types of people, right where they were. Therefore, we simply cannot rightly understand God's plan of redemption, the life and ministry of Jesus, or the work to which Jesus now calls the Church, apart from a profound appreciation for the role of service.

Serving Compassionately

In modeling a life of service, Jesus established a pathway for his followers that runs in complete contradiction to that of our broken world. Although the world seeks to usurp dominion, gain status and seize power, the disciples of Jesus set their sights on this work of service. In so doing, they strive not only to restore relationships between humanity and God, but also to bind the wounded and feed the hungry.

It would, of course, be presumptuous to claim that we as Christ's followers are called to the same work of redemption through servant-ministry that he so consistently portrayed. It would be presumptuous, were it not for context of that crucial verse in Mark 10:45. A crisis of ambition among the disciples had finally come to a climax, and two of them made a bid for preeminence. James' and John's request to sit at the right hand and left hand of Jesus in heaven put them at odds with the others. Jesus, rather than seeking to create a compromise among the egos of these twelve individuals, used the opportunity, not only to reveal his mission, but also to call his disciples to follow his example:

> When the ten heard this, they began to be angry with James and John. So Jesus called them and said to them, 'You know that among the Gentiles those whom they recognize as their rulers lord it over them, and their great ones are tyrants over them. But it is not so among you; but whoever wishes to become great among you must be your servant, and whoever wishes to be first among you must be slave of all.' (Mark 10:41-44)

Seeing the example of Jesus and the clear command of Christ to follow in this pattern places the issue of compassionate service squarely before everyone who claims to be his disciple.

News had reached the northern frontier town of Deerfield in the Massachusetts colony, informing the people to anticipate an attack from the north. For several months they waited, but nothing happened. It snowed early that year, so no one expected an army to cross 300 miles of rough frontier and attack them now! On the night of February 29, 1704, snowdrifts began to form. The snow fell gently and the watchman slept. The drifts grew against the town's outer wall, forming a huge ramp. Without warning, two hundred Indians and French soldiers rushed over the walls and entered the town. The slaughter that followed was ruthless and widespread; men, women and children perished.

Some survivors were taken captive and gathered in the newly occupied house of John Sheldon. Cold and bleeding, they huddled together. A young French officer, wounded in the fight, lay dying in another part of the room. One of the captives, Mary Catlin, who had just lost her husband and two sons in the battle, arose at his call and gave him a cup of water. Her neighbors criticized her for caring for the killer of her family. Quietly she replied, "If thine enemy hunger, feed him. If he thirst, give him drink." Perhaps not surprisingly, Mrs. Catlin was subsequently freed by her astonished captors and spared the ordeal of traveling 300 snow-filled miles with the other captives north to Canada.[4]

Such a willingness to serve even our enemies stands in stark contrast to the heart and actions of this unredeemed world, but it is in perfect harmony with people who claim to follow Jesus. From the world's perspective, Mrs. Catlin's actions were abnormal. Who could possibly look upon the killer of her husband and children and willingly choose to serve them? Who could possibly demonstrate such compassion to the least worthy of individuals? Only a person whose heart has been filled with the love of Jesus Christ. Only a person whose heart has embraced a radically new set of values.

Such values were regularly taught by our Pietist forefathers (see the Introduction). In the third point of *The Pia Desideria* ("Pious Desires"), no doubt the "Manifesto of Pietism," the Pietists insist that "more attention should be given to the cultivation of individual spiritual life. Love for God and man should take priority over theological disputes." "Knowledge," they continue, "is secondary to practice."[5] In their minds, to know the importance of serving on Christ's behalf, yet fail to do so, is an unreconcilable contradiction.

One simply cannot fail to serve and still claim to be right before God (cf. James 4:17).

Serving at the Point of Need

Given the nature of his ministry and his increasing notoriety, Jesus regularly encountered many people with a great variety of needs. Mark describes one such encounter in this way:

> A leper came to him begging him, and kneeling he said to him, 'If you choose, you can make me clean.' Moved with pity, Jesus stretched out his hand and touched him, and said to him, 'I do choose. Be made clean!' Immediately the leprosy left him, and he was made clean. (Mark 1:40-42)

On this particular occasion early in Jesus' ministry, an unnamed leper approached him. Being a leper at that time and in that society meant loneliness and desperation. Lepers typically lived together in a colony of sorts outside the flow of the community. Social contacts were extremely limited, and even participation in religious activities was forbidden. Seemingly separated from both people and God, many lepers undoubtedly wished to die.

Under these conditions, Jesus represented the man's best hope. Unfortunately, no self-respecting rabbi would dare come into contact with anything or anyone unclean, let alone a leper. Still, when given the rare opportunity, the man fell before Jesus and begged. Surprisingly, Jesus not only heard the leper's cries, but actually answered them. In the exchange that immediately followed, Jesus served this broken and previously ignored man at precisely his point of need.

But how does one know what the point of need is? In some cases, such a need is immediately obvious. Jesus surely had little difficulty determining what to do for the begging leper. However, on other occasions areas of need might be hidden or concealed by other less important matters. Furthermore, we might readily slip into the trap of assisting people based on our own agendas rather than their actual needs. Again, how do we know what the area of genuine need is? How did Jesus know?

Being Present

First, Jesus knew the needs of people he served because his heart was open to them. There is at times a human tendency to distance ourselves from the very people we are called to help. Jesus refused to do that, choosing instead to face these people head on. He walked with them and spoke with them. In fact, virtually all of his acts of service occurred during the ordinary routines of his life. For us to serve in equally appropriate and helpful ways, we too must move about among hurting people and be vulnerable enough to them so that we experience a God-given compassion.

I recall one experience in my own life when the truth of this struck me with great force. I was working in a soup kitchen when an otherwise unknown man walked in. He was dirty and reeked of an unpleasant combination of odors that probably resulted from not bathing, sleeping in a dumpster, and smoking whatever noxious plant was available. As he lifted his empty bowl, I noticed chipped fingernails and hands covered with a black filth. Our eyes did not meet. Ashamed of his wretched condition, he waited with his head facing the floor. I ladled the soup into his bowl and, with a smile, said, "God bless you." At the sound of the soup and the words of blessing, he lifted his gaze, looked into my eyes and smiled. In that moment, we shared the common experience of being two people for whom Christ died. No longer was this smelly man just a hand with an empty bowl.

Touching

Second, Jesus discerned areas of genuine need because he dared to touch even the unclean people he served. Jesus might very well just have spoken a word to the leper, but he realized that more than that was needed. This isolated, dirty and diseased man probably longed for someone to touch him and extend to him the powerful reconnection and exchange that comes with physical contact. Drawing strength from the relationship with his Father and concerned entirely with obeying his will, Jesus was unafraid of becoming disconnected, dirty or diseased. Jesus was a servant determined to assist even the dirtiest individuals.

Our service must follow this same pattern. Without being foolish and naive, we must be willing to allow the pain of others' wounds and disconnections not only to touch our hearts, but to move our hands. Likewise, our service must flow from a vital relationship with the Father and a deep commitment to do his will in all things. In doing so, we too can address the needs that stand before us in a spiritually empowered and physically tangible way.

Listening

Finally, Jesus recognized the deepest needs of people because he paid attention to them. The prophet Isaiah drew a fascinating connection between ministry and listening in one of his Servant Songs:

> The Lord God has given me
> the tongue of a teacher,
> that I may know how to sustain
> the weary with a word.
> Morning by morning he
> wakens—
> wakens my ear
> to listen as those who are taught.
> (Isaiah 50:4)

Jesus might very well have said these same lines.

An interesting episode from the Gospel of Mark stands out in this regard. Although the person he serves never speaks, Jesus demonstrates an uncanny sensitivity to the situation. In short, he pays careful attention. On the occasion in question, four men worked feverishly to dig a hole through the clay roof of a house. First, they used tools; then, as the clay began to break, they got down on their hands and knees and tore away large chunks of clay and straw. Using ropes, the four persistent men lowered their friend down to the feet of Jesus. Noticing the cripple before him, Jesus surely saw a twisted and disabled individual. Yet, as he looked into the faces of the invalid and his friends, he discerned something. He sensed in them a profound belief that he could actually do something for them. Once again, no one said a word; the "problem" was obvious. But Jesus quickly recognized that something more than a word of physical healing was needed. As a result, he addressed a deeper but far less obvious need: "Son, your sins are forgiven" (Mark 2:5).

From this story and the Servant Song in Isaiah 50, we see that the gift of an instructed tongue, which brings help to the weary, comes first through opening our ears. It's easy for us to assume from outward appearances and our own prejudices that we know exactly what needs are present. But our assumptions often fail to touch a person's deepest and most pressing need. We must learn to listen, both to God and the people around us.

In his book entitled *New Seeds of Contemplation*, Thomas Merton describes a Christianity that is devoured by activities and strangled by attachments. He observes the existence of Christian leaders who fear the solitude of listening, do everything possible to avoid it, and draw others "into activities as senseless and as devouring as their own."[6] Obviously, we can hardly approach the needs of others unless we first listen to them. Less obviously, but more profoundly, we cannot powerfully address the needs we hear and observe unless we have listened as servants to the Lord.

Serving Sacrificially

I had never heard of Floralba Rondi before. She was a nun who had spent most of her seventy-one years ministering in a clinic in Kikwit, Zaire. Sister Floralba Rondi was also the first of many nuns who served as medical workers to perish in the 1995 outbreak of the Ebola virus. I read the story in a weekly news magazine with a sense of personal dread, not out of fear of the horrible disease that killed her, but because of implications that her death raised in my heart and mind. According to the article, "The missionaries of Kikwit provide the only semblance of social services in a town where the government exists mainly to extort money."[7] Here was a woman who, along with her Christian co-laborers, had devoted her entire life to Christian service. What troubled me was the fact that I only now heard the name of Sister Floralba Rondi because she had been killed by a famous disease!

Deep in thought, I leaned back in the chair in my office, a small 220-square foot rented room that served as the work space for myself and another man in the church. All our other church equipment sat in a 1970 GMC pickup truck, covered with an old donated camper shell in my driveway at home. Again and again, the thought ran through my mind, "How many other Sister Rondis are out there? People who expend themselves in the service of Jesus and who won't die by an internationally known and feared virus?" Equally frightening, I wondered about my own dreams for recognition and acclaim. I certainly never wanted to stay in a ministry that failed to outgrow the walls of a small office and housed its equipment in the back of an old truck. What would I do if God called me to such a life of service, to spend my entire life, silently and faithfully serving Jesus in some backwater town without any recognition? Such a life—one that denies wealth and notoriety— runs counter to everything my North American culture has taught me.

The fact that service generally has a positive reputation in our culture failed to calm my fears. Such groups as the Peace Corp, VISTA or Americorps, not to mention various professional service groups like Rotary, Kiwanis, and the Lions, are understandably viewed as positive activities by our society in general. In a culture that is increasingly self-oriented, the value expressed in helping others continues to be seen as good and noble. Accordingly, even non-Christian parents often raise their children to understand the value of temporarily putting aside self-interest to help others.

This is not, however, the type of service undertaken by Floralba Rondi, nor is it what members of the Brethren in Christ Church had in mind when they placed a towel and basin on our logo. As helpful as volunteering with such organizations might be, Christian service involves far more than a temporary diversion from whatever else we may do with the rest of our lives. It is not a vacation spent helping others, but a life given away. While reading that newspaper account, I suddenly realized how costly serving Christ can be. "It is," as Thomas à Kempis wrote so long ago, "a great honour, [and] great glory to serve Thee, and to despise all for Thy sake."[8] Or as Howard Snyder wisely observes,

> We are called to be cross-bearers more than cross-wearers... the cross means voluntarily choosing to live our lives for others, letting the life of Jesus show us what true spirituality is.[9]

The ministry, life and sacrificial death of Jesus bound the life of service inextricably to the cross. As a result, we cannot separate Christian discipleship from costly, cross-bearing service.[10] Not only are we called to set aside our time, energy and resources for the service of God and his kingdom, but to die to them.

In 1991, we gathered at the graveside of a young woman named Jennifer Lenhert. Jennifer was only 19 years old when she left her Brethren in Christ community in North America to serve with a missions group in Kenya. Before long, she contracted a severe form of malaria and died. Now, her family and friends joined together in a deep yet hope-filled grief at her passing. As I stood by the graveside, I thought how the kingdom of God had advanced because of such sacrifice and devotion. I even wished for my daughters and son nothing less than to bear the cost of Christian service and to pour themselves out for Christ's sake. The eternal rolls of God's people are marked by those who shouldered the cost of service and bore it willingly with grace and dignity, more often than not in utter obscurity. Among our own people, when "dear old brethren [who] walked and rode on horseback hundreds of miles, visiting and preaching the word of God,"[11] they served their Lord at the cost of everything else. It was a servant's heart that led the likes of Alice Heise, Frances Davidson, Jesse and Elizabeth Engle, and Barbara Hershey to spend themselves on the continent of Africa serving the lost. Christian service by its very nature is extremely costly.

Serving Collectively

As we have already seen, personal piety reveals itself in costly and lasting service, particularly to the poor and the powerless. If this is true, then communal health and vitality will similarly express itself in a united heart to help others in Christ's name. As Brethren in Christ, all three of our traditions—Anabaptism, Pietism and Wesleyanism—arrive at the same conclusion: the visible community of believers is a serving community (see the Introduction).

Service is both an inward function and an outward force. Our obligation to serve starts within the context of the community of believers. Here, any number of scriptural directives regarding care for our brothers and sisters stand in force.[12] Here, among those with whom we share our most intimate relationships, we first demonstrate the love of Christ. Within the community of faith, service which is quietly and unpretentiously performed out of love for Jesus is a means to draw other believers closer to him. Through service, we bind, heal, and build others up in the faith.[13]

The world makes vain attempts at attaining this type of unity through means other than God's way. Prior to the 1996 Olympic games, the International Olympic Committee chairman, Juan Antonio Samaranch, was interviewed. He said that by putting on the Olympic games, he was doing something "more important than the Catholic religion."[14] The bombing that took place that year at the Atlanta games only further marred the image of a peaceful union that is the facade of the Olympic movement. The reality is that the Olympic games have been a place where competing societies can find a different way to express their ongoing tensions and hostilities. In spite of the boastful efforts of Samaranch and others, the tensions and hostilities remain.

A successful communal life expressed through humble service stands as a witness to a world which is constantly attempting but consistently failing to draw people together. Christian service growing out of a redeemed heart is a dynamic expression of love, and stands as a powerful witness to the world of Christ's redemptive might (i.e., John 13:35).

Service taken beyond the Christian community is also an outward force. Through Spirit-directed acts of service, the witness of Jesus goes forth in direct and fresh ways. A church that actively engages in outward acts of service cannot be easily dismissed as socially and culturally irrelevant. Rather, such a church will increasingly find itself on the cutting edge of human need.[15]

Conclusion

Greatness in the kingdom of God does not come through power and prestige, but through surrender, humble service and acts of love (Eph. 4:2; Gal. 5:13). Like the woman in Bethany who lavishly anointed the Lord with costly ointment, so too are the people of God called to serve the hurting and needy of the world today (Matt. 26:6-13). Christian service, however, does not flow from nor is it dependent upon human resources, but upon the power of God in the lives of individual believers and the community of faith as a whole. A healthy Christian community will evidence its vitality, not only in numbers saved or prayer vigils held, but in servants sent and deeds of righteousness accomplished. Such service only comes at great cost through lifelong commitments to do the work of Christ in the world. This kind of vibrant and faithful obedience to God will always mark a people as peculiar and powerfully relevant.

Discussion Questions

1. In what ways has "the Fall" in Genesis 3 distorted peoples' views of work and service?

2. In following the example of Jesus, what specific acts of service have you personally engaged in?

3. Since becoming a Christian, in what areas, if any, have you seen an increasing heart for service in your life? Specifically, where and in what form do you sense a burden for the needs of others?

4. Discuss the implications of "being present" and "touching" with respect to service. How might these concepts affect where we go and who we spend time with?

5. Has a fear of harm or sin ever kept you from practicing acts of service? Where and when? How does God's call to overcome evil with good come into play?

6. What personal costs would you experience if you followed Christ's call to service?

7. How important is discerning the voice of God in our service? How do we hear God's voice, and is listening primarily passive or active?

8. In what ways has your church successfully modeled Christian service, and how could this model be developed and expanded?

9. What practical steps can we take that would help make lifelong service for Christ preeminent in our lives?

10. How has Christian service in your community resulted in an effective witness for Jesus?

For Further Reading

Campolo, Anthony. *Ideas for Social Action*. Grand Rapids, Mich.: Zondervan Publishing House, 1983.

Deen, Edith. *Great Women of the Christian Faith*. Uhrichsville, Oh.: Barbour and Company, 1959.

Foster, Richard. *Celebration of Discipline*. San Francisco: Harper and Row, 1978.

Smith, Timothy L. *Revivalism and Social Reform*. Baltimore: Johns Hopkins University Press, 1980.

Viv, Grigg. *Companion to the Poor*. Monrovia, Calif.: MARC, 1990.

8

Pursuing Peace

We value all human life and promote
forgiveness, understanding, reconciliation,
and nonviolent resolution of conflict.

by Harriet Sider Bicksler

Whoever of you loves life, and desires to see many good days...
Turn from evil, and do good; seek peace and pursue it.
—The Psalmist (Psalm 34:12, 14, NIV)

In early 1918, as World War I intensified, Canada needed to strengthen its armed forces and started drafting all young men, aged 20-23 years. There were no exceptions. One young Brethren in Christ man, Ernest Swalm, had strong convictions that the Bible's call to nonresistance and peacemaking included non-participation in war.[1] When the letter came demanding that he report for duty, he did not resist the order. However, when he arrived in Hamilton, Ontario, at the appointed place and time, he refused to put on a military uniform and requested to be allowed instead to do humanitarian service that would not help to support the war effort. For his refusal, he was arrested and put in jail where he remained for four months.[2]

More than 70 years later, in the period between Iraq's invasion of Kuwait and the Persian Gulf War in early 1991, Gwen White, a pastor's wife from Riverside, California, traveled to Baghdad, Iraq, with a delegation called a Christian Peacemaker Team. The team's aim was to promote nonviolent resolution of the conflict. Gwen carried with her messages of peace and friendship from her son's sixth grade class to the children of Iraq. When she returned home, she wrote about her "unlikely journey." Reflecting on her experience in Iraq, Gwen called her readers to "choose to gain our security from God and not from weapons, and then may we speak from that position for peace."[3]

Ernie's and Gwen's methods of witness against war in favor of pursuing peace were different, probably reflecting the times in which their witness took place. While both confronted those who were making war, Ernie did not resist the order to report for military duty. He simply refused all other orders to participate in the war-making system. Gwen, by way of contrast, confronted her government more directly by openly traveling to an enemy country.

At the same time, their witness had common elements as well. Both Ernie and Gwen desired peace and believed that God wills peace and not war. They believed they were doing the right thing and what God wanted them to do. They both were opposed to war and participation in war, and they both demonstrated love for their enemies. For Ernie and Gwen, pursuing peace was a core value. It was something they had to do, regardless of the consequences and whether or not they were successful, because of their deeply-held beliefs about the nature of God, what it means to follow Jesus, and how God wants us to live in the world.

Pursuing peace is certainly not just about opposing war, as these two stories might suggest. But I'm telling the stories to make a specific point. It is easy and common for almost anyone to say that he or she wants peace—who doesn't? But it is not so easy or common to believe that Christians can practice—and boldly give witness to—life-saving and life-giving alternatives to conflict and aggression. It is not easy because the culture we live in assumes that violence and war are acceptable solutions to aggression, and the majority of the Christian church basically agrees. Undaunted by prevailing opinion, however, the Brethren in Christ actively promote forgiveness, understanding, reconciliation, and nonviolent alternatives to conflict and war.

The Brethren in Christ belief in the importance of pursuing peace is more than 200 years old. Peacemaking has always been part of our understanding of the gospel of Jesus Christ. The gospel is good news, and peace is also good news. We celebrate and share it with the world. We know everyone wants peace, and we know something about how God can help us be peacemakers, so we are not shy or apologetic about sharing what we know. After all, there is a world out there that clearly hasn't been particularly successful at achieving and sustaining peace.

What exactly can we share with the world? What do we believe about peace and why? In this essay, I intend to summarize our long-standing understandings about pursuing peace, including what we believe the Bible says about peacemaking. Then I will explore each part of our eighth core value to show what it means to pursue peace. Finally I want to challenge us to be assertive about sharing this part of God's good news with the world.

What We Believe

The earliest Brethren in Christ confession of faith declared that it is "completely forbidden to use the sword for revenge or defense."[4] Our current confession says that "Christ loved His enemies and He calls us as His disciples to love our enemies. We follow our Lord in being a people of peace and reconciliation, called to suffer and not to fight."[5] These brief confessional statements show that the Brethren in Christ understand the Bible and the example of the early church to teach that war and violence are wrong responses to conflict, and that love, even for enemies, is the right and ultimately most effective response. Although God in the Old Testament appears to condone and even promote violence, what with all those stories of sending the people of Israel into battle against enemy nations, the Brethren in Christ have placed more emphasis on the life and teachings of Jesus as the culmination of God's revelation to his people. Even in the Old Testament, however, there are clear teachings that point to a different way to respond to violence.

God repeatedly reminded the people of Israel that they were not to trust in their own strength or in military might for their deliverance: "A king is not saved by his great army.... Truly the eye of the Lord is on those who fear him..." (Ps. 33:16ff), or "Alas for those who go down to Egypt for help and who rely on horses, who trust in chariots...and in horsemen...but do not look to the Holy One of Israel or consult the Lord" (Isa. 31:1). The concept of loving enemies was introduced in the Old Testament where the writer of Proverbs talks about feeding hungry and thirsty enemies (Prov. 25:21-22), and God said that revenge should be left to him. The prophets foretold how Jesus as the "suffering servant" would model meekness and absorb violence, and provided visions of the future when nations would not learn war any more but would beat their swords into plowshares (Isa. 53; cf. Isa. 2:3-4 and Mic. 4:1-4).

The bottom line for me and for many Brethren in Christ in terms of the biblical basis for peacemaking has always been the example of Jesus. Try as I might, I can't imagine Jesus pushing the button to release a bomb, firing a gun at someone, or engaging in a knock-down, drag-out fistfight with an adversary. This is not to say that Jesus didn't vigorously confront evil and wrongdoing; in fact, he overturned the tables of the moneychangers and condemned the Pharisees for their hypocrisy and self-righteousness. But I just can't imagine him deliberately hurting or killing another human being.

From before his birth to the time of his death, Jesus proclaimed peace. Zechariah, speaking of Jesus at the time of his own son's birth, talked about the one who would "guide our feet into the way of peace" (Luke 1:79). The angels, on the night of Jesus' birth, declared peace on earth and goodwill to all (Luke 2:14). Jesus' most famous sermon blessed peacemakers, calling them God's children, and pointed to a different way to deal with enemies and people who hurt us and demand things from us (Matt. 5). At the time of his arrest, Jesus didn't fight back, reprimanded Peter for cutting off a soldier's ear, and told Pilate that because his kingdom was not of this world, his disciples wouldn't fight to protect him (John 18:36). Paul and Peter, in their letters to the churches, instructed their readers to live at peace with everyone, overcome evil with good, follow the example of Jesus who did not retaliate or threaten when he was attacked, and seek peace and pursue it (Rom. 12:17-21; 1 Pet. 2:21-23; 3:10-11).

Jesus' witness and example were so powerful that for almost 300 years, Christians did not go to war, and for 2,000 years, at least some Christians have continued to believe that war and violence are wrong. One example is Origen, an early church leader, who said, "we no longer take up 'sword against nation.' Nor do we 'learn war any more,' having become children of peace, for the sake of Jesus, who is our leader."[6] With roots in the Reformation, the Historic Peace Churches, which include the Brethren in Christ, have maintained a commitment to peace and nonresistance despite the fact that most of the rest of the Christian church has moved away from this same commitment.

What Pursuing Peace Involves

We have defined "pursuing peace" to mean that "we value all human life and promote forgiveness, understanding, reconciliation, and nonviolent resolution of conflict." Each part of the statement addresses a different aspect of the pursuit of peace. Together, they portray an approach to life with enormous potential for good in the world.

"We value all human life..."

The statement begins with the rather bold declaration that "we value all human life." The "all" word is the challenge. Do we really mean all human life—the murderer on death row; the ruthless dictator who massacres his own citizens while amassing great personal wealth; the unborn baby conceived by a rape; the homeless alcoholic who won't accept help; the nasty coworker who is always criticizing? Surely there are limits! We haven't allowed ourselves any escape clauses, however.

We know that God created all human beings in God's own image, and we believe that humans are special in a way that other parts of God's creation are not (Gen. 1:26-27). Now we have to figure out what it means to have the image of God in us, and what that implies about how we treat other people, regardless of how they may have perverted that image within themselves.

Among other things, it is not enough to say we value all human life and still think there are circumstances where it is appropriate to take human life deliberately. Is there ever a point when we can determine that someone has forfeited his or her right to be treated as a person made in the image of God? To do so seems to decide that an individual is beyond God's reach and beyond redemption, and hence to decide that he or she cannot and will not ever choose to accept God's offer of grace. Perhaps the choice will never be made. Perhaps the person has already made so many evil choices that a good choice is impossible, but no one except God can ever know that for certain.

Practically, then, this means that as a Christian I can't support the death penalty. I can't participate in activities that demonize people for bad things they've done or choices they've made, or because of their race, the country in which they live or their religion. I can't participate in war on the one hand, and I can't condone abortion, infanticide or euthanasia on the other hand. I can't do these things because I value *all* human life.

"...and promote forgiveness..."

Jesus' life was premised on forgiveness. He willingly died on the cross so that we don't have to pay the penalty for our sins. He forgave those who participated in his crucifixion and death. He taught his disciples to pray for forgiveness and to extend it to other people, warning that if we don't forgive others we shouldn't expect God to forgive us. Recognizing that forgiveness is not a once-and-done thing, he said that we should forgive the same person for the same thing over and over again (Matt. 18:21-22).

Just what is forgiveness, though? As a non-theologian, my definitions are fairly practical, beginning with a simple dictionary definition that says forgiveness means giving up resentment against or the desire to punish. It doesn't say anything about forgetting or pretending the wrong never happened. Forgiveness also doesn't happen easily, just because I say the words. Forgiveness doesn't dismiss responsibility or the need for people to be accountable for their actions, and doesn't mean that I am not careful about how much I trust people who have shown themselves to be untrustworthy.

But forgiveness, it seems to me, also means that I don't forever hold people's misdeeds over their heads as a club, always reminding them of what they've done wrong. Forgiveness means that I don't seek revenge, or wish evil on those who have done bad, even really awful, things to me or to people I love. Forgiveness helps to break the cycle of violence, whether the violence is physical and literal or more emotional and subtle. Forgiveness doesn't necessarily change the person I forgive (although it may very well do so), but it changes me and allows me to let go of the desire for revenge and punishment. Harboring resentment uses up energy that could be directed to more productive and loving activities.

The difficulty of forgiving becomes very real when we consider actual people who may need our forgiveness: the father who sexually abused his daughter for years and still refuses to admit he did anything wrong; the person who brutally murdered a family member and has been sentenced to death by the state; the drunk driver who caused an accident that resulted in permanent paralysis; the bully who constantly threatens a child; the coach who cut a child from the basketball team and damaged his self esteem; the church member who constantly criticizes and hurts others with her negative and complaining spirit. Forgiveness for these and countless other situations is probably not possible on our own. Forgiveness requires us to allow God to work in us to release the normal anger, pain, resentment, and desire for revenge we feel when we are wronged.

"...understanding..."

The word "understanding" has several meanings. The ones that apply in this context are sympathy or empathy and tolerance or respect. To begin to understand others, we need to listen to them, hear their stories, and learn to know what it is like to walk in their shoes. Understanding takes time. Understanding also values the person, recognizing the image of God in him or her. Understanding recognizes the many factors that influence a person's character, personality and actions. The person who always seems to criticize everything may have experienced much criticism as a child. The person who is having a really bad day at work may be going through a rough time at home. The person who seems to have reached the point of no return by committing brutal crimes may never have known what it was like to have someone love him or her unconditionally. So often we condemn without knowing or even wanting to know the life circumstances that contributed to the bad choices people make.

This does not mean that to understand we have to excuse bad behavior or limit accountability. It certainly seems like this is what frequently happens in the courts, as people who have committed horrible crimes "get off" with very little punishment because juries are convinced by defense arguments of childhood abuse or whatever. Understanding doesn't mean we don't require people to take responsibility for their behavior or its consequences, but it ought to mean that we learn to know where people came from, what made them what they are, and why they act as they do. That kind of understanding, then, ought to help us develop caring relationships with people that will give us the right to prod them to be responsible. It also ought to help us determine the root causes not only of one individual's behavior but also of societal and cultural behaviors, and perhaps help to prevent the hatred, violence, and war that come from lack of understanding.

Another aspect of understanding that promotes peace and prevents violence is tolerance. Although tolerance seems to have fallen into some disrepute lately because we keep being asked to tolerate behavior we think is wrong, at its core it is another word for respect. We can and should tolerate and respect people and their beliefs even when we don't agree with them. Lack of tolerance leads to hate crimes, violence, and war far too often. Tolerance and respect, on the other hand, help to create an environment in which understanding and eventually reconciliation can more easily take place.

"...reconciliation..."

When the bank and I don't agree on how much is in our checking account, I have to reconcile the difference. Sometimes this means that I find a mistake in subtraction or addition or I've forgotten to record a check or a withdrawal, and sometimes (although not very often) it means the bank made a mistake—like the time they inadvertently printed our account number on someone else's checks and our balance all of a sudden began to dwindle. When I can't find the reasons for the discrepancy, and it's not obvious that the bank has made a mistake, I usually assume the bank is right and I change our balance to agree with theirs. I put aside my differences and agree that from this point on the bank and I are in agreement.

I think reconciliation between people and groups works in a similar way, although no analogy is without limitations. Ideally, reconciliation is more two-sided than in my checkbook example, with all parties agreeing that mistakes were made and from now on we will work to correct those mistakes. Yet God provided for our reconciliation to him with no initial reciprocal action on our part. "While we were still enemies, Christ died for us," Paul says in Romans 5. But Paul also says that God reconciled us to himself through Christ and then entrusted us with the ministry of reconciliation as well (2 Cor. 5:18-19). God made the first move and now it is up to us not only to accept his offer of reconciliation, but also to extend reconciliation to others.

Part of extending reconciliation to others is making peace with people from whom we are estranged, which is possible because of what God has done for us. The classic biblical example of this is in Ephesians 2, where Paul describes how Christ made peace between the Jews and the Gentiles, two groups that had traditionally been in conflict with each other. Christ broke down hostilities and created one new humanity, reconciling "both groups to God in one body through the cross" (Eph. 2:14-17).

The conflict between the Jews and the Gentiles and the model for reconciliation described in Ephesians 2 have many potential parallels in our modern world. Long-standing ethnic, racial, religious and national hostilities can be broken down through the power of Jesus. People who were formerly strangers and foreigners can become friends; they can be reconciled. That's a major part of the message of the gospel. When we participate in or stand silent in the face of actions that perpetuate hostilities and conflicts among people and nations, we are denying an essential truth of the gospel that Christ came to make peace and reconcile people to God and to each other.

One North American opportunity for reconciliation is between races. When North America was settled centuries ago, indigenous peoples were displaced and large numbers were killed. There's something incredibly wrong when some of the poorest people with the greatest social problems in the United States and Canada are descendants of people that white settlers treated with so little understanding and respect.

Similarly, the legacy of slavery and racism continues to create hostility between the dominant white culture of the United States and people of other culture and races. Racial reconciliation means coming to terms with the stark reality that discrimination and prejudice against people still happen just because of the color of their skin or they are different in some other way. For white people, who still hold most of the power in the United States, it also means accepting responsibility for the privileges we have for no other reason than that we are white and working to make sure that everyone has the same privileges. Racial reconciliation leads us one step closer to John's vision in Revelation of "saints from every tribe and language and people and nation" singing together in heaven (Rev. 5:9).

"...and nonviolent resolution of conflict."

One time when my daughter was a young child, we were watching a TV movie about World War II. As we watched, she became increasingly bothered by the story and eventually blurted out, "War is dumb! Why can't they just talk?" I've thought about that a lot in the years since. I have my own moments of excruciating frustration when I hear war stories from around the world or local news stories of an angry husband who shoots his wife and children and then turns the gun on himself. Obviously, preventing war and violence is not usually as simple as my daughter's suggestion to "just talk" makes it sound, but on the other hand, it seems like nations and people assume far too quickly that violence is the only way to solve a problem.

I like to use another analogy. We are quick to point out the irony of a parent beating a child for hitting his or her brother or sister. We recognize the incongruence between the words and the actions. But we are not nearly so quick to see that we often condone the same thing when we assume that violent behavior can only be stopped with more violent behavior, which is what happens in war or capital punishment. Granted, there are major differences in the complexities of the situations, but it's sometimes helpful to put aside all those complexities and look at a situation very simplistically. If we can see that a parent who beats a child for hitting is continuing the violence, perhaps we can see that trying to resolve violence on a larger scale with more violence also simply perpetuates violence. The best solution is to decide never to use violence, which is at least part of what the early Brethren in Christ meant when they said rather categorically that "it is completely forbidden to use the sword for revenge or defense." Without a sword (or a gun) in the home, or a state-of-the-art bomb in the national arsenal, physical violence is not as easy an option, and there is more likelihood that other methods, like my daughter's call for "talking," will be used with more vigor and desire to make them work.

I can't leave this section without acknowledging that violence is not always physical. Emotional, verbal, and social violence are also very real and can often be equally devastating. In addition, just because we have prevented war or another violent act may not mean that we have achieved genuine peace and reconciliation. Often preventing war is just the first step in a long process of establishing a climate in which real peace can happen. Logic tells me, however, that if people are not killed there is a greater likelihood that forgiveness, understanding, and reconciliation can in fact take place.

Conclusion and Confession

When I was beginning to think about this essay, an editorial headline in our local newspaper about the decades-long Middle East and Northern Ireland peace processes caught my eye: "Pursuing Peace is Trying." The editorial used the word "trying" in the sense of difficult, time-consuming, and patience-wearing. Pursuing peace is certainly all that. But the editorial also suggested a second meaning: pursuing peace is a continuous process of trying to make things right, trying to reconcile even when the odds seem stacked against the process. Just because it doesn't work this time doesn't mean that we don't try again and again and again.

For the Brethren in Christ, having the pursuit of peace as a core value also means trying to reinvent our commitment to peacemaking and reconciliation in ways that are relevant to the age and culture in which we live. I said at the beginning that the message of peace is something to embrace, celebrate, and share. Instead, we often hide it for fear of ridicule or rejection, or because there is strong disagreement about the finer points of what the Bible actually teaches. Rather than focus on fears and disagreements, however, we can act on what we have always said we believe. If we do so, we will go out into the world committed to being peacemakers wherever we are. The world and our neighbors and friends need to know that we really believe and have faith that through Christ and his death and resurrection, we and they can have the power to overcome evil with good. Jesus Christ not only provided for our personal salvation; he also gives us power to be peacemakers and his agents of reconciliation in the world. Jesus showed that there is another way that genuinely respects God's image within each person, regardless of race, nationality, creed, or behavior.

Let me close with a little personal confession. Pursuing peace in the ways I've described is a high value for me and one that I have worked at all of my adult life because I believe in the deepest core of my being that God calls Christians to peacemaking. Having said that, I am also painfully aware that I have not always acted as though I believe it; I have not always practiced forgiveness, understanding, and reconciliation. Further, I know that there are often more questions than answers about what peacemaking really means (some of those questions are raised at the end of the chapter), and I know that many sincere Christians who also take their Bible seriously have come to different conclusions about war and peace, and violence and nonviolence.

However, by choosing the word "pursuing" to describe what we want to do about peace, we are acknowledging that it is a continuous activity. We are always going after or chasing peace. Sometimes peace is elusive, sometimes there are complications, sometimes there are obstacles to overcome. Maybe we will never quite capture peace, but we are always pursuing, always following after Christ, who indeed is our peace and will be always be with. This has been and continues to be my goal as a pursuer of peace, and I pray that it will be yours as well.

Discussion Questions

1. Reflect on the different ways Ernie Swalm and Gwen White expressed their commitment to pursuing peace. Discuss other ways they could have resisted their governments' war-making.

2. Define peace, peacemaking, pacifism, nonviolence, and non-resistance. Which of these words do you prefer and why?

3. Although the Brethren in Christ have always believed that peacemaking and nonresistance are expressions of Christian faith, during the past 50-75 years there has been less agreement in the church about this part of our doctrine. Even our confession of faith now recognizes differences of opinion (see note 5 on p. 182). Does this bother you, or do you appreciate belonging to a church that recognizes varying points of view in the Christian community? Explain your answer.

4. Why does it seem like we often fight about peace? Why are discussions about peacemaking, pacifism, nonresistance, or nonviolence often so difficult?

5. How would you answer the person who objects that pacifism and nonresistance are ineffective in the face of an evil as great as the Holocaust?

6. What do you do to overcome evil with good and to break the cycles of violence in your world?

7. This essay has not included any consideration of the Christian's responsibility to government. Consider the tension between believing that Jesus' call to be peacemakers means being opposed to participation in war and other state-sponsored killing (e.g., the death penalty) and also believing that Christians are instructed to obey their government.

8. The words "peace" and "justice" are often used together, and it's often said that without justice there is no peace. How and why is this true? Think about places in the world where injustice has contributed to violence and war.

CONTEXT	TYPE OF CONFLICT; HOW MANIFESTED	PEACEMAKING RESPONSE
Personal		
Home		
Community		
Job		
National		
International		

9. Someone once said, "Let the Christians of the world agree that they will not kill each other." Reflect on the statement, especially in light of the conflicts in many places in the world that pit Christians against each other. How much difference would such an agreement make?

10. I once developed a peacemaking continuum that named six contexts for peacemaking: personal (within myself), home, community, job, national, international. For each context, I named the types of conflict and peacemaking responses. Based on the pursuing peace core value, and the ideas of forgiveness, understanding, reconciliation, and nonviolent resolution of conflict, flesh out the continuum. Reflect particularly on the importance of being a peacemaker across the continuum, and not just at one end or the other. A format is provided above.

For Further Reading

Augsburger, Myron S. *The Peacemaker*. Nashville, Tenn.: Abingdon, 1987.

Peace and Justice Series. Scottdale, Pa.: Herald Press. Fourteen different titles available, including the following:
  Barrett, Lois. *The Way God Fights*. 1987.
  Byler, Dennis. *Making War and Making Peace*. 1989.
  Franz, Marian. *Questions That Refuse to Go Away: Peace and Justice in North America*. 1991.
  Redekop, Vernon. *A Life for a Life: The Death Penalty on Trial*. 1990.

Schrag, Martin H. and John K. Stoner. *The Ministry of Reconciliation*. Nappanee, Ind.: Evangel Press, 1973.

Schrock-Shenk, Carolyn and Lawrence Ressler, eds. *Making Peace with Conflict: Practical Skills for Conflict Transformation*. Scottdale, Pa.: Herald Press, 1999.

Yoder, John Howard. *What Would I Do?* Scottdale, Pa.: Herald Press, 1992.

9

Living Simply

We value uncluttered lives, which free us to love boldly,
give generously, and serve joyfully.

by Esther Spurrier

Thank God for the things that I do not own.[1]
—*Teresa of Avila*

Several years ago I helped some friends load up their possessions to move to another state. As the day went on, we carried box after box of stuff out to the truck. Soon, my friends began to express great dismay at all they had accumulated while living for seven years in that house. They now confess that this moving experience profoundly affected their resolve to begin simplifying their lives.

Anyone who has lived in the same place for a period of years knows that we tend to collect far more than we realize. But is accumulation entirely bad? The friends I spoke of above owned an amazing collection of tools and gadgets. Any tool you might want for any job you needed to do could be found in their house. They were also incredibly generous, however, with their own time, expertise and possessions if anyone needed help.

Stuff. Sometimes it seems to take on a life of its own and even reproduces without any effort from us! Furthermore, if we're not careful, taking care of all our stuff can become very time-consuming, adding to the clutter of our lives. If we say that we value uncluttered lives, perhaps our first task is to look carefully at what causes us to clutter our lives and what it is that clutters them.

Cluttering our Lives

In my grandparents' day, living took a great deal of physical effort. People worked hard on their farms, grew or raised and processed much of their own food, made clothing, and built houses and barns. Then "creative" people began to invent and manufacture tools, machines, and appliances that made life much easier. Now it seems there is a tool or appliance for any job we might need or want to do, and the fact that these are available makes them seem necessary. Therefore, the most obvious reason we clutter our lives with things is to gain more comfort, control, or convenience.

A second reason we clutter our lives is our need for significance. In contemporary society, our income, possessions, and accomplishments seem to determine our status. If I want to be regarded well, a high salary, nice house, and new car are good places to begin. If we want to give our children a good start in life, we are pressured to provide the latest toys, fashionable clothing, and enriching activities. We must, at all costs, "keep up with the Joneses." And if we somehow resist these societal pressures, we often fall prey to a more subtle one. We fill our lives with work, meetings and activities so we will be thought to be productive members of society and even the church. I am not a wage-earner, and people, especially those in the church, often ask me what I do with all my time. They are concerned that I not be lazy or unproductive.

A final reason our lives become cluttered is the large number of choices and opportunities that face us each day. The array of products—all made to do the same thing—require us to spend time and energy sorting out which one is best. Children begin early making choices in our society. They decide what they want for Christmas, what they're going to be when they grow up, what clothing they will wear to school, which of the many sport and activity opportunities they are going to be involved in, and which course of study to pursue. And have you noticed how nearly every conference you attend these days has a number of workshop options from which you can choose? Choices and options have of course enriched our lives, but they also pose a danger of cluttering them with complexity.

The question confronting us, then, is how can we as brothers and sisters in Christ effectively unclutter our lives while we live in an increasingly wealthy, busy, and complex society? We look first in the place we've always looked for guidance in how to live out our faith in the world. We look to the Bible, which gives us help for simplifying our schedules, our stuff, and our speech.

Simplifying Our Schedules

In the very beginning of the Old Testament we see God as creator of the universe, of all that is in our world. He is also revealed as the author of time and all of its rhythms:

> And God said, "Let there be lights in the dome of the sky to separate the day from the night; and let them be for signs and for seasons and for days and years, and let them be lights in the dome of the sky to give light upon the earth." And it was so.
> (Gen. 1:14-15)

Later, after God finished with his work of creation, he rested and inaugurated a day of rest (Gen. 2:2-3). Time, with its rhythm of work and rest, is a gift from God.

Our family spent more than a decade living in a rural part of Zambia in Africa. My favorite part of the day was evening. I loved the beauty of the sunset with the trees silhouetted against the sky and the twinkle and smoke of the cooking fires. But more than the beauty, I loved the fact the evening truly signaled the end of the day's activities, the beginning of a time of rest. Since travel was by foot and snakes were more of a danger at night, people did not move around much after dark. Even churches did not generally schedule evening meetings. This was a novel blessing for one who had grown up in a North American pastor's family, when evenings were often filled with church activities.

Night was only the first of God's provisions for rest. Just as he rested after his labor of creation, God commanded his people to observe one day in every seven as a holy day of rest (Exod. 20:8-11). Furthermore, the Old Testament designates one year in every seven as a sabbath year for God's people. During that year, the land was allowed to rest from its labor of producing food (Lev. 25:1-7).

Today, technology enables us to circumvent these natural rhythms. Electricity and modern transportation allow people to work at any time of the day or night. Chemical fertilizers enrich the soil for growing crops. At the midpoint of the 20th century, analysts were even predicting that a 30-hour work week would soon be the norm! Nevertheless, people are now working more hours rather than fewer, and recent health reports warn that modern people are not getting enough rest.[2]

Interestingly enough, both society and science are beginning to acknowledge the truth in God's plan. Recently, one New England state considered reinstating its "Blue Laws," which had earlier prohibited businesses from operating on Sundays. Legislators apparently grew concerned about the lack of time families had together. In addition, many centuries after God gave the Law to the people of Israel, agriculturalists announced the wisdom of allowing land to lie fallow to be renewed for crop production.

We also see God's pattern of work and rest echoed in the life of Jesus. While he preached and taught, healed and cared for a great many people, we sense no frantic urgency in his ministry. He often went off by himself or with some disciples for prayer, solitude, and rest (i.e., Matt. 14:22-23; 21:17; Mark 1:35; 4:35; Luke 6:12; 9:18, 28).

We don't unclutter our schedules for selfish reasons, but rather to develop intimacy with God and others. An old gospel song we sang when I was a child said, "Take Time to be Holy." Recently a missionary returning to North America from a less time-oriented country confessed that he was struggling with the busyness of our society, sensing that it was not nurturing in him a life of personal holiness.

Uncluttering our schedules also frees us to assist others in the routines and crises of their lives. When someone comes to me with a need or request, I am often tempted to say, "I don't have time." On other occasions, I fulfill the request grudgingly, feeling pressured by other obligations. I have been challenged by brothers and sisters in whose lives I see modeled joy in serving. In his advice to young Christians, the apostle Paul encourages them to live lives of love, making the most of every opportunity to live as children of light in a dark world (Eph. 4–5). If this is true for young Christians, how much more do mature Christians need to leave spaces for those opportunities to happen and to seize them eagerly. Can I leave empty spaces in my schedule, anticipating that God will bring divine interruptions my way?

Simplifying Our Stuff

The second area of our lives that often cries out for simplification involves our property and possessions. Once again, the Bible provides more than enough guidance for us to think through the issue carefully.

Giving Generously

The same chapters in Ephesians that talk about making good use of our time also speak about giving generously. Paul writes that those who have been stealing should begin working, not so they will better their own lives by their productivity, but so they will have something to share with people in need (Eph. 4: 28). If recovering thieves are to act like this, shouldn't all of God's people be sharing the fruit of their labors with others? The apostle John even states that sharing with those in need is an essential indicator of the love of God in Christian people (1 John 3:17).

When we look back to the creation story, we find that God gave humans the work of partnering with the Creator by helping each other and caring for the world (Gen. 1:28ff). After Adam and Eve sinned, work became more of a burden, focused on personal survival (Gen. 3:16-19). Later, working to amass personal wealth apparently became a problem, because God instituted a "Year of Jubilee." During that year, the poor received back their family lands or their freedom which they had had to forfeit (Lev. 25). And in the wisdom literature of the Old Testament, we find many warnings about the dangers of riches (i.e., Prov. 25:16; 16:18; 23:4-8).

A common belief held today asserts that prosperity is a sign of God's blessing, to be unashamedly displayed by Christians. When God called Abraham to leave his land and his people to follow God's direction to another place, he made a covenant with him. God promised that he would make childless Abraham into a great nation, that he would bless Abraham and make his name great, and that all peoples on earth would be blessed through him (Gen. 12:1-3). We do well to remember that when God blesses people with spiritual and material blessings, they are not to dam the flow into a reservoir of treasure for themselves, but are to channel those blessings to others.

What has it meant for God's people to live as sharing people? We find in the New Testament that sharing was a part of the practice of the early church. People sold some of their possessions so they could help others (Acts 2:42-47; 4:32–5:11). New church officers (deacons) were chosen to channel help to people in need (Acts 6:1-6). The generations of Christian people who followed found it imperative also to respond to human need beyond their own churches and communities. Missionaries were sent out across oceans into dangerous cities and underserved rural areas to teach and preach, to heal and help. Drought and famine in Eastern Europe early in the twentieth century gave rise to Mennonite Central Committee, the relief and development arm of the Mennonites and Brethren in Christ, which continues to function today all over the world.

The biblical model and the example of previous generations continue to guide and challenge us today. When my husband was in medical school, I joined the spouses' auxiliary, which functioned as both a fund-raising/project-promoting organization for the medical school and a support group for lonely family members adjusting to the demanding working hours of their spouses. During one meeting we got into a discussion of the problems of raising children on a doctor's income without their becoming spoiled brats. Perhaps naively but very sincerely I suggested that we could just give away a good portion of our income so we wouldn't need to deal with the problems of excessive wealth. The suggestion fell flat, not gaining a response from anyone. Maybe they thought I wasn't being serious.

Later we would find out how difficult it actually is to live this way. Excess income is very seductive, and we found it challenging not to keep raising our standard of living, not to spend more and more on ourselves, as our income rose. Increasing our giving did not solve all of the problems either. When the children asked us to buy something for them that we felt was excessive, we couldn't just say, "We can't afford that." We had to say, "We don't choose to use our money that way." And that brought all sorts of opportunity for hurt and disappointment.

The assaults of advertising add to the difficulty of living simply. Ads make us aware of new products and cause us to want more things. Perhaps it is important for us to consider ways we can protect ourselves and our children from the seductions of advertisements. One young mother in our church shared that she had to begin throwing away the catalogues that arrived in the mail without looking at them because they made her want things she knew the family didn't need.

The differing attitudes toward money and possessions my husband and I brought from our families of origin created conflict in our relationship, but also helped us work toward a conscious plan for our family. We knew that both sets of parents had hearts for God and his work, and it helped to see that honoring and serving God with what we have could be lived out in different ways. What seems like thrift and wise use of possessions to one person may seem selfish or extravagant to others. Perhaps the lack of hard-and-fast rules for possessing stuff makes it difficult for us to unclutter effectively. Having a plan for acquiring and using things, however, helps us set boundaries.

Clinging Nervously

Possessions can be alarmingly attractive. What is it about them that often interferes with our living for God? One concern is that the accumulation of things insulates us from our need for God. After the children of Israel escaped from Pharaoh through the Red Sea, they began to grumble and worry about how they were going to survive in the desert. In response, God sent them food from heaven every day, but they were to gather only what their family would use in one day (except on the sixth day, when they were to gather enough for the Sabbath so they could rest from their gathering on that day!). Any excess food they tried to hoard became rotten and wormy (Exod. 16). The Israelites had no choice but to trust God, though many did not trust very joyfully.

Jesus echoes the same value of trusting God in the Sermon on the Mount (Matt. 6:25-34). In potential conflict with his teaching, our society is very forward-looking. We are encouraged to plan for every emergency and stockpile resources for our retirement. Doing so seems so right and natural that we often don't give it a second thought. Many Brethren in Christ of my grandparents' generation, however, did not invest in insurances. Even putting lightning rods on barns was considered by some as showing a lack of faith in God. Their retirement plan consisted of raising children who would care for them at the end of their life. Church communities were committed to helping each other in times of need and emergency. These practices now may seem quaint and naive, vestiges of a time long past when people lived in the same community all their lives and knew each other well. But we do well to think about how much is enough with regard to these purchases and whether we are showing a lack of trust in God by our dependence on insurances and retirement plans.

A second concern is that possessions can hinder us from following God's leading. Before John and I accepted the invitation of Brethren in Christ World Missions to go to Zambia, our plan had been to go to an underserved area of the United States. Here we could both serve the church and, importantly, have our medical school debt forgiven. It seemed like wise planning and good stewardship. But the larger plans of the mission program negated our plan and led us to Africa. Now, long after that fork in the road, we see the wisdom of God and the benefit to our family of abandoning our plan and following God's.

When we later returned from Zambia in 1987, we knew we would likely live in Pennsylvania for awhile, so we bought a house. At the time I remember a vague uneasiness about whether this place would someday feel like bondage if God opened the way for us to return to overseas service. We now stand at the threshold of that opportunity, and one of our big concerns is what to do about the house. We can become sufficiently connected to our stuff that it inhibits our willingness to follow God freely.

A third concern is that proper care for the things we own uses time and energy. There is nothing wrong with caring for our possessions unless it takes too much time or keeps us from being generous with what we have. From time to time my husband and I have talked about investing in rental property, but then we realize how much time and energy are already consumed in taking care of the house we live in. We don't need any more to care for, anything more to focus our attention on ourselves.

We do need a continual reminder that we are merely caretakers of our possessions and that they have been given to us so we can share with others. In his new book, *Mustard Seed vs. McWorld*, Tom Sine quotes Robert Kaplan as saying that

> material possessions not only focus people toward private and away from communal life but also encourage docility. The more possessions one has, the more compromise one will make to protect them.[3]

When I was young, the pastor often reminded the congregation before the offering was taken that "all we have is God's, and we give it out of his hands." I find that reminder ringing in my head to this day—an important truth to remember when society is prizing personal acquisition.

Years ago our family developed a relationship with a family who had no outward or active practice of faith in God. Their willingness to share what they had with others made a deep impression on me. My tendency was to be protective of my balloon-tire bicycle, telling the children it was my "work vehicle." I also struggled when people asked to borrow the bike for fear it would get damaged. In contrast, Mr. Bruce-Miller gave our son his first driving lesson. He also taught the children to navigate his outboard motorboat among the dead trees of Lake Kariba, even though this risked damage to his equipment that was not easy to repair or replace in Zambia. His example continues to be a challenge to me; as a Christian I should be much less absorbed by and selfish with my possessions.

Lastly, the accumulation of riches in this world may dull our vision and anticipation of the very real heavenly reward that Jesus promises to all who believe (John 14:1-6). Did you ever notice how many songs about heaven were written by people who were experiencing trouble, hardship, or loss? For many of us, the possibilities for longer life and high-tech medical care are increasing, and we are experiencing an attitude in society which says that whatever is technologically possible is necessary. Rather than planning ahead for an uncluttered end of life that allows for healthier human relationships and an excitement about being with the Lord, we tend to cling to our earthly lives.

My husband works as an emergency care physician, so he deals with life and death decisions often. He has noticed that families in conflict have a much more difficult time letting a terminally ill relative die than do families where there is harmony. Keeping relationships open and loving, and refusing to let the sun go down on our anger (Eph. 4:26), may be a way to prepare for an uncluttered end of life. It is also very important to have our desires for medical intervention at the end of our life written and available to those who will care for us. Finally, even in death we can share our still-useful body parts with others for whom this gift might mean renewed life and health.

No One is Exempt!

Those of us who struggle to make ends meet may be thinking that simple living is an area we need not work on; our lives are uncluttered to the bare bones! But people who don't have much or who are burdened with debt may also find their time, energy and very thought life consumed with money and possessions. One woman recently told me that not an hour passes that she doesn't worry about her family's precarious financial situation. For such people, focusing on God and his provision and care is vital. Allowing brothers and sisters to help and advise is also crucial. And we need to remember that generosity is an attitude of the heart, with little correlation to what is given or the amount. The Old Testament story of the widow who shared her last bit of food with Elisha (2 Kings 4:1-7) and Jesus' calling the disciples' attention to the widow's very small offering (Mark 12:41-44) are testimonies to this truth.

During our years in Zambia I was touched and challenged by the daily expression of generosity and hospitality from people who did not have much in the way of material possessions. One of the best gifts I've been given was several inches of warm water in the bottom of a large galvanized tub in which I could bathe after a dusty motorcycle ride to a village on a hot day. Knowing that the women had to walk far to get the water, then carry it home, and heat it over a wood fire, made me feel very humble and thankful. As I talk to people from other parts of the developing world, I find these are common practices. Generosity may flow in one direction at a particular time, but those who have received material help may be able to give back to their benefactors or help others in different ways or at another time. These activities not only meet a practical immediate need, but they serve to cement relationships among people as we learn to know and are known by others.

Simplifying Our Speech

A third area of challenge with regard to uncluttering our lives concerns the way we speak The Bible commands us not to give false testimony (Exod. 20:16), to put off falsehood, and to speak the truth (Eph. 4:25). It is certainly true that lies create webs which complicate life and destroy people. But there are other ways our speech becomes cluttered which may hinder our service to God.

Jesus reminds us to be clear and direct with our "yesses" and "nos" (Matt. 5:37). We shouldn't need to complicate our speech with protestations of honesty to those with whom we haven't always been straightforward, with jargon that keeps others from understanding, with ways of wording things that mislead or cloud an issue, or with reasons or excuses. When I lived in Zambia I came to realize that when someone asked me for something, all they expected in response was a simple yes or no. I didn't need to come up with a reason, explanation, or excuse. These are things our society expects, especially if we are refusing a request. You may think that sounds too easy, but I found that this practice forced me to consider more carefully what God would have me do with regard to these requests. Rather than focusing on the expectations of the person asking or on my personal situation, I found my thoughts often going to the words of Jesus, "Give to everyone who begs from you, and do not refuse anyone who wants to borrow from you" (Matt. 5:42).

Complexity of speech can also affect our prayer life. When I was a girl, I was impressed with two different kinds of prayer. The first was the prayer of my grandpa at mealtime. His prayer was long and involved but always the same. Any one of us grandkids could have repeated it verbatim—maybe some still can! Though it amused us, we were also touched by the spiritual concern he had for each of us as he brought his family to God. The second kind of prayer was the truly poetic and eloquent praying we heard from some of our church fathers. Although it was beautiful to hear, it made me feel like I could never pray well enough to pray aloud in church. Jesus speaks about uncluttering our prayer life by coming to God in humility, trust, simplicity, and a forgiving spirit (Matt. 6:5-13). Does my prayer life, even all of my public spiritual life, encourage others to become more involved, or does it smack of an exclusivity that only a select few can attain?

Uncluttering the Church

So far we have looked at what we as followers of God can do to unclutter our personal lives. But if we believe that the church is somehow more than just a conglomeration of individuals, that it is in a mysterious way the body of Christ, how can we unclutter our life together to enable us as a body to love boldly, give generously, and serve joyfully?

Just as individuals struggle to live godly lives amid the lure of the world's value system, the body also struggles against the current in a society that flows with such values as bigger is better, you get what you pay for, big business has the best model, and variety is the spice of life. I visited Prague this past summer and was struck by the contrast between the elaborate cathedrals and the simple churches founded by followers of reformer John Huss. The ancestors of our church fathers and mothers experienced those reformation changes and brought with them a concern for simplicity. Early Brethren in Christ met in homes and later began to build simple meetinghouses. Their dress was plain, modest and distinctive, marking them as separate from the world.

In an effort to reach out and grow in the latter half of the twentieth century, our denomination has let go of rules about dress and appearance. Congregations have tried to discover the needs of their members and communities and have planned church programs and buildings accordingly. As churches have grown, this has meant a multiplicity of options for different ages and genders, working and non-working groups. We have traditional, contemporary, and blended worship services. And those who carry the responsibility for leadership, both paid staff and volunteers, often feel like they're still not doing enough to care for and appeal to everyone. I looked in our church bulletin this week and counted fifteen activities on the weekly calendar in addition to small groups, Sunday school, and two worship services!

In each age and generation the challenge remains to present the gospel in fresh and meaningful ways. Yet it is very hard to decide to discontinue programs that may have outlived their effectiveness, and so our church calendars get fuller. Also I sense a longing in some places to step back from the many specialized programs to fewer worship and discipleship experiences, but ones that include a broader range of people. What might it mean for your congregation to unclutter itself corporately?

In the early decades, denominational structure was fairly simple. Pastors were chosen by "drawing straws" among a number of candidates the congregation had discerned were worthy. Any one of the several preachers could be asked to preach on a given day, so all needed to be prepared. As clusters of churches grew up, a bishop was selected to oversee the district. These churches might come together for special meetings, such as baptisms and the "love feast," a multi-day meeting which included communion and foot washing.

As the denomination has reached out and grown, leaders have struggled to find structures which best meet the administrative needs of a larger body. A number of different models have been tried and fine-tuned. The trend has been toward a more centralized structure. Whether one views this new centralized structure positively ("integrative") or negatively ("bureaucratic"), leaders must always seek ways of encouraging a sense of connectedness, even among the far-flung congregations, regions, and international conferences of the denomination.

During the gathering in which these ten core values were identified, some participants expressed strong sentiment that final editorial changes be left to the Leadership Council, the administrative group which includes the bishops, general church administrators, and agency executives. But the general church leaders' strong commitment to the whole-group process carried the day, and the group stayed and worked on details until participants were satisfied that the job was done. Conscious or unconscious, this cooperative effort likely helped create a broader ownership of the values across the church than might otherwise have been true.

What principles can help us as we plan church facilities and activities? The most obvious is to ask whether God is glorified (Matt. 5:14-16; 1 Cor. 10:31). I greatly appreciate our earlier concern for simplicity, and our years in Zambia reinforced that appreciation for simple structures. But perhaps we have neglected opportunities to glorify God through aesthetic beauty. A second issue is faithfulness to God's call. Does this program help us warn and encourage each other to faithful and holy living (Heb. 10:23-25)? Does it help us share God's truth with others (Matt. 28:18-20)? Thirdly, unity is a theme that pervades Jesus' prayers during his last days on earth (John 17:20-23). Does this decision of our congregation or denomination help connect us to the larger body of believers? Are we working together to spread the good news of the kingdom of God, or are we being competitive and territorial? And lastly, we need to be investing our resources in ways that bring spiritual treasure that lasts forever (Matt. 6:19-21). Our buildings and programs will crumble, but the body is eternal. Is it rooted in love, grounded in God's Word, reaching out to share with others and enfold new believers, and growing in holiness?

Conclusion

Is there an antidote to clutter as we work at simplifying our schedules, our possessions, our speech, and our life together in the church? In dealing with the material world, people take extreme positions. Ascetics and some followers of eastern religions deny the material world, saying there is no good or truth in it. Western society has pronounced the material world very desirable and encourages us to give in to our desires at every turn. But for the Christian, the key must be in focusing on God. Jesus reminds us that the eye is the lamp of the body (Matt. 6:22), able to fill the body with light or keep it in darkness. There is no such thing as a divided focus; we cannot serve both God and possessions. The writer to the Hebrews expresses the same idea in this way:

> Therefore, since we are surrounded by so great a cloud of witnesses, let us also lay aside every weight and the sin that clings so closely, and let us run with perseverance the race that is set before us, looking to Jesus the pioneer and perfecter of our faith, who for the sake of the joy that was set before him endured the cross, disregarding its shame, and has taken his seat at the right hand of the throne of God (Heb. 12:1-2).

Keeping our eyes on Jesus' life and example and focusing on

serving God, personally and corporately, help us to decide where and how to unclutter our lives. As Richard Foster so aptly states it,

> When we focus on God, we will embrace certain truths: that our stuff has been given to us by God, that it is not ours to hold on to, and that it is intended for the good of the larger community. That perspective results in simplicity.[4]

Discussion Questions

1. What exercises of devotion and spiritual intimacy with God have helped you keep your focus when busyness or possessions threaten to cloud your vision?

2. Is it true that there are no hard-and-fast rules for what a Christian should or should not acquire? Are there any general principles which guide your life as you consider buying things or adding events to your schedule?

3. An older woman in our community celebrates her birthday by asking her guests to bring donations for the local food pantry rather than gifts for her. Are there other ways we can celebrate holidays and special anniversaries in a manner that encourages sharing rather than cluttering?

4. Communal living has been a way for some Christians to share resources and nurture relationships. Are there aspects of shared ownership we could practice in our churches today?

5. What might uncluttering look like for one who is forced to work several jobs to make ends meet or one who is deeply in debt? What responsibility do we have for each other in the church in situations like this?

6. In earlier days, church members used to ask wisdom from each other in deciding whether or not to make some major purchase.

Would such a practice be a good idea in our day and age? Might it also help us to better handle the lure of advertising?

7. Can someone in your group talk about what is involved in making a Living Will, which deals with end-of-life decisions? How can such a document be a testimony of faith in Jesus Christ?

8. More and more schools are adopting uniforms as a way of helping students focus on academics rather than fashion. Do Christians need encouragement to dress simply and modestly? How could this be accomplished?

9. Just as an empty day or hour on my personal calendar allows the Spirit a space to breathe into me, so may white spaces in our church bulletins allow the breath of God to fill us as a church. Are there ways you can unclutter your life as a congregation?

10. A growing denomination seems to need a more complex administrative system. How can we foster connectedness and intimacy as a denomination without sacrificing growth?

For Further Reading

Chester, Leonard J. "What About Modesty and Simplicity?" *Evangelical Visitor* (Sept/Oct 1999), pp. 4-6.

"God and Your Stuff." *Discipleship Journal* (Jul/Aug 1999), pp. 37-68.

Foster, Richard J. *Freedom of Simplicity*. San Francisco: HarperSanFrancisco, 1981; reissued 1998.

Sider, Ronald J., *Rich Christians in an Age of Hunger*. Dallas: Word, 1977; revised 1997.

Sine, Tom. *Mustard Seed vs. McWorld*. Grand Rapids: Baker Books, 1999.

10

Relying on God

We confess our dependence on God for everything, and seek to deepen our intimacy with him by living prayerfully.

by Jay E. McDermond

*If we think that a little prayer can't do any harm,
we will soon find that it can't do much good either.
Prayer has meaning only if it is necessary and indispensable.*[1]
—*Henri J. M. Nouwen*

Having arrived at this book's final chapter, we notice a significant shift. Whereas the previous core values begin "We value…," this last point reads "We confess our dependence on God for everything, and seek to deepen our intimacy with him by living prayerfully." We are astutely aware of the enormous task presented by the first nine core values. Who, in their own strength, can open themselves to "the transforming power of the Holy Spirit"? Who, in their own strength, can be wholeheartedly obedient? Who, in their own strength, can be a consistent "active and loving witness for Christ to all people"? Who, in their own strength, live "uncluttered lives"? The very fact that core values one through nine employ the active verb "we value" hints, at the very least, at the fact that while we may set biblical authority, heartfelt worship, and integrity in relationships as our goals, we may not always live unswervingly at the high level we desire. There will be times when we fail to serve others, promote forgiveness and reconciliation, or live up to any of the other core values. In fact, without God's help we cannot even begin to live the lives reflected in these core values.

Therefore, we must "confess our dependence on God for everything and seek to deepen our intimacy with Him by living prayerfully." This final chapter explores two topics. The first focuses on Jesus Christ's relationship to God and the Holy Spirit and how that impacts our attempts to live prayerfully. The second topic explores practical ways we can nurture lives of dependence on God.

Prayer and the Ministries of Jesus

The broader Christian church, including the Brethren in Christ denomination, has long believed that Jesus of Nazareth was God in human form. The opening chapter of John's Gospel tells us that Jesus, the Word, was with God and was God from the beginning of time. When Jesus was born he was both fully God and fully human. In John 1:18 we are told that one of Jesus' goals in life was to make known to us the God we have never seen. Through the history of God's interactions with Israel, humans were given partial glimpses of God's nature, but we did not receive a full revelation of God until Jesus lived among us. In his life we learned of God's true nature, and Jesus revealed God's actual identity because he was God.

But more than this, Jesus was also human. In the Gospels we read that Jesus experienced the same things we frail humans experience. He was born a baby. He grew up and went through adolescence. He was tempted. He was thirsty. He cried at the death of his friend Lazarus. And he himself died. Jesus clearly, according to the Bible, understood what it meant to be human. As a result, only Jesus of Nazareth was able to comprehend two very different experiences: divinity and humanity.

It is this uniqueness which is the foundation for the first aspect of Jesus' great ministry begun in the first century A.D. and continuing today. In his living he showed us what it means to be truly human creatures made in the image of a holy God. His life modeled the holiness to which we are called. This calling involves humility before God, loving God and our neighbors, living lives dedicated to service and reconciliation, openness to the transforming power of God, and living intimately with God. In essence, our lives are to reflect Jesus' life.

But we humans face a serious problem. We are, in our own power, incapable of living like Jesus. We cannot imitate his model because we are weak and sinful creatures, and we are unable to conquer our sinfulness. It is at this point that Jesus offers us a second ministry. He takes upon himself the sin of the entire world, including our individual sin, offering himself as a sin sacrifice to God. Whereas people in the Old Testament relied on animal sacrifices to remove human sin, Jesus, in obedience to God, gives himself once and for all as the sacrifice for our sin. No longer are animal sacrifices needed because Jesus, God's Son, has died for all human sin, thus breaking sin's power in every human's life. Whereas before we were hopelessly bound by the power of sin, we are now free to respond to God's call through Jesus' death on the cross.

Not only are we set free from sin, but God also gives us a solid hope of transformation in Jesus' resurrection, which is a third aspect of his ministry. We need not continue in sin only to be forgiven. The Christian life does not have to be an endlessly repeating cycle of sin, forgiveness, sin, forgiveness. The Resurrection is God's testimony that we can be transformed by the divine power which overcame both sin and death and resulted in Jesus' new resurrection body. When we accept that Jesus Christ died for our sins and was raised to new life, we are bound together with him, or as the apostle Paul says, we are "in Christ" (2 Cor. 5:17). We become new creatures. Our past is just that—the past. In Christ Jesus we are free, and we have hope for the transformation of our lives.

A fourth ministry which occurs through Jesus Christ is often missed. This ministry focuses on his ascension. We are told in Luke 24:50-53 and Acts 1:9 (cf. John 20:17) that after his resurrection, Jesus Christ was taken back up into heaven to be with God the Father. We realize that he sits in heaven at God's right hand, but I suspect we often miss the reason why this is so. Hebrews tells us that Jesus Christ sits with God functioning as our high priest. He goes before us into God's presence (Heb. 6:20) and draws us near to God, interceding for us (Heb. 7:25-26). The risen Christ is the perfect intermediary because being divine he understands God and having been human he understands us. His primary roles as the ascended Lord are to plead our case before God and to translate our weak and flawed prayers to God. When we pray we do not pray alone. Jesus Christ is beside God praying with us and on our behalf.

Not only has God acted in the past through Jesus Christ, but God also gives us the Holy Spirit, the Spirit of Jesus Christ. Left to our own resources we could not understand God's will nor would we have the power to carry it out. But this has been made possible through the Spirit's presence in our lives. In John 14–16 Jesus promises his disciples that we will not be alone once he returns to the Father. The Spirit is given in order to maintain our connectedness to Jesus and the Father. The Spirit also helps us live as Jesus lived. This is especially clear in Acts. There the disciples receive the Holy Spirit and they then proceed to do the exact same activities that Jesus did in his earthy life.

In all of life humans are dependent upon God's grace. This is also true for our spirituality and our desires to live prayerfully. Without God's initial gracious work in Jesus Christ and the continued ministry through Jesus' Spirit, we could not develop an intimate relationship with God. It seems clear that this assumption and our faith in God's gracious activity on our behalf impacts the way we look at and understand our intimacy with God. As we have seen above, Jesus Christ, through the Holy Spirit, has opened the way to God for us and is ready to enable our journey.

James B. Torrance tells a story which neatly sums up this section. In California as a lecturer at Fuller Theological Seminary, he had gone to the beach for a swim. Just as he was about to enter the ocean, he greeted an elderly gentleman who was walking pensively along the beach. As Torrance finished his swim, the gentleman spoke to him again, asking where he was from. Torrance explained that he was a Scottish Presbyterian minister on a lecturing and preaching tour of the U.S.A. The elderly man's face lit up and he exclaimed, "How astonishing that I should meet you just now!" He told Torrance of how his wife was dying of cancer after their 45 years of happy marriage. Furthermore, his father had been a devout man and a Presbyterian minister who faced the death of his wife with confidence, faith, and prayer. But this was not the elderly gentleman's own current experience. He had drifted away from the church, and despite his desperate attempts to pray and find hope over the past several days he had failed. Torrance writes,

> What did I say to him? Did I tell him how to find faith and how to pray—throw him back on himself? No, I did not. I said, "May I say to you what I am sure your father would have said to you? In Jesus Christ we have someone who knows all about this. He has been through it all—through suffering and death and separation—and he will carry you both through it into resurrection life. He has heard your cry for faith and is answering." I continued, "You have been walking up and down this beach, wanting to pray, trying to pray, but not knowing how to pray. In Jesus Christ we have someone who is praying for you. He has heard your groans and is interceding for you and with you and in you."[2]

Within three days Torrance met with both the man and his dying wife, leading them back to Jesus Christ. He concludes this story with these words, "The first real step on the road to prayer is to recognize that none of us knows how to pray as we ought to. But as we bring our desires to God, we find that we have someone who is praying for us, with us, and in us."[3] How correct he is. Our first agenda is to remember that we never pray alone. Jesus Christ, God's own son, has opened the way to God, and he prays with us through the Holy Spirit making our concerns known to God and conveying God's will to us. This fundamental truth must take precedence over issues of "how" to pray. The question is are we willing to do what is necessary to take advantage of this access to God. The deepening of our intimacy with God involves our attempts at nurturing a life of dependence on God. This does not happen automatically simply because God has made it a possibility. And with this truth in mind we now turn our attention to the chapter's second focus: practical concerns relating to our life with God.

Deepening Our Intimacy with God through Prayer

In his classic book, *Celebration of Discipline*, Richard Foster writes, "Prayer catapults us onto the frontier of the spiritual life. Of all the spiritual disciplines, prayer is the most central because it ushers us into perpetual communion with the Father."[4] Foster's reason for this claim is simple and true. Real prayer is God's way of changing us and creating in us a life which is transformed and Christlike. It is in the process of praying that we meet God and open ourselves to the Holy Spirit's leading us to imitate Jesus Christ. For this to happen prayer must be "much more than throwing a bag of words at God," as I once heard an Anglican monk critique the popular view of prayer, or simply praying for others, as important as that is.

Waiting on God

To be perfectly honest, "prayerful waiting" is very difficult. The theological traditions which influence our denomination rightly value and hold up "doing" as a virtue. This is seen clearly in the previous core values. Many of the core values use action verbs. Others employ words indicating what we are to do. We read phrases such as "study it," "build our lives," "integrity in relationships," "an active and living witness," "serving others," "promote forgiveness," "love boldly," and so on. Additionally, our culture tells us we are most useful when we are busy. Who among us does not have more than enough to do? We have come to believe that to be involved and active is to be faithful.

And so Henri Nouwen is correct when he writes, "Waiting is not a very popular attitude."[5] Often it is equated with a lack of focus or simply wasting time. But just the opposite is true. To run from meeting to meeting, social event to social event, and activity to activity reveals our true lack of focus. Many of the events filling our calendars and days are taking time away from more significant endeavors which have eternal value. Ultimately, we are religiously and culturally conditioned to lead busy lives which keep us from the one activity and person who can give us true meaning and focus: prayerful waiting with and listening to God.

I suspect there is one central reason why we do not regularly pray with a view to being transformed. In our heart of hearts we are afraid. We do not want to give up our routine behaviors. They are ours. They give our lives meaning. They are who we are or at least who we want people to think we are. If we do give up our old patterns and values, what will replace them? What will we become? Will people still appreciate us? And most threatening of all, prayer is being open to God. Who does not fear what God might think of our innermost thoughts and desires? As Nouwen writes,

> Praying is no easy matter. It demands a relationship in which you allow someone other than yourself to enter into the very center of your person, to see there what you would rather leave in darkness, and to touch there what you would rather leave untouched. Why would you really want to do that?[6]

Why indeed? Because of our fear we fill our lives with noise, worthwhile activities, worthless activities, recreation, and work. We will do almost anything to avoid the fear that comes with changing into the people we are called to be under God's guidance. Frequently we will do anything to escape working with God in the task of self-examination, and so we elude God and prayer. But God loves us too much to allow us to remain the same as we are today. It is to our advantage to allow our compassionate and loving God to work at our transformation through prayer.

An initial and fundamental assumption for all types of prayer, but especially true for the specific form about which we are concerned, is that we must learn to be conscious of God's presence in our world and lives. This will not happen if our lives are filled with busyness and clutter. It will not happen if "devotions" are just another thing to do on our already long list of "things to do." We must take serious time to be silent and listen for God's voice. As Elijah learned, God rarely screams at us. Instead, whispers are often God's way of communicating (1 Kings 19:12-13). While it is true that God desires a meaningful relationship with us and uses many ways of communication, I am convinced that time spent alone and in silent listening is the most beneficial. We must establish this form of prayerful communication before we can begin to hear other forms, such as through creation, other people, the circumstances of our lives, journaling, or even dreams.[7] God wants to communicate with us intimately; the question is, are we willing to be quiet and listen?

A second and equally crucial question is how does God speak to us? What is the medium through which we hear God's voice? As we have seen in chapter 2 of this book, from the beginning the Brethren in Christ Church viewed Scripture as central for understanding both Christian faith and practice. We believe our spiritual formation and grasp of the faith is tied to the Bible. Given this fact, I would suggest that our "living prayerfully" must also focus on Scripture. It just so happens that the larger body of Christ has time-honored approaches to prayer which look to the Bible as the primary way through which God speaks to believers. It is to our advantage to consider these biblical prayer forms.

Praying with the Bible

A very basic approach to prayer using the Bible is found in the second chapter of Jeanne Guyon's devotional classic, *Experiencing the Depths of Jesus Christ*.[8] Guyon lived in late seventeenth century France, and her small book led to both her fame and imprisonment. God used her writing to kindle faith all over France, but the Roman Catholic Church had grave doubts about its usefulness. After her death, her ministry continued through her written legacy. Among those who read *Experiencing the Depths of Jesus Christ* and benefitted from it were the early Quakers, Count Zinzendorf and the Moravians, John Wesley, people in the "Holiness" movement of the late 1800s, and Watchman Nee.[9]

The second chapter of her text identifies a wonderfully simple approach. She called it "Praying the Scripture." Guyon assumed that God still uses Scripture to speak to people, and so one reads the Bible with a view to finding God's focus for one's prayers. She suggested a person quietly and humbly approach a selected small passage of Scripture. You read this passage *slowly* and *carefully* in an attempt to "*sense*" the very heart of what you have read."[10] Once you "sense" the passage's core meaning you make that topic the focus of your prayer. After a time of prayer on this subject you go to the next small passage and repeat the process. The ultimate goal of "Praying the Scripture" is "to find the Lord in what you are reading, in the very words themselves."[11]

George Carey, the Archbishop of Canterbury, with strong evangelical roots, regularly listens to passages from the Bible as part of his prayer life. In his sermon entitled "Prayer—a Two-Way Conversation," Carey shares a personal illustration in which a phrase that he had recently "listened to"—Philippians 4:6—helped transform both his heart and his behavior:

> About six months ago I was very cross with a colleague who had, in my opinion, acted irresponsibly. I remember approaching the theological college quite determined to "sort him out." As I approached the college the phrase from this passage: "in everything by prayer and supplication with thanksgiving" flashed through my mind. I started to meditate on that verse in relation to my argument with my colleague. I imagined God saying something like this: "So you are going to sort him out, are you? Begin with thanking me for him; look at him as a person as important to me as you are." I did so. I started to thank God for this colleague of mine and his gifts and commitment. As you will have guessed, my attitude towards him changed, so that when the frank speaking happened that day it was in the context of love and acceptance of him as a person.[12]

I myself have been using this approach to prayer, and have also found it to be a significantly positive addition to my intercessory prayers. In fact, it has brought a new and deeper dimension to my prayer life. Previously I had found it difficult to read Scripture in a "devotional" fashion. I was not sure what I was looking for in the process of reading. Additionally, I sensed that I was responsible for generating or identifying what I was to pray about in my quiet times. But Guyon's assumption that I read slowly and carefully to hear God speak to me has given me a goal and provides the focus for my prayers. Hearing God speak through the Bible has given me a specific form for the familiar A.C.T.S. acronym for prayer. God, through the Scripture, suggests why he should be *adored*, indicates what I need to *confess*, reminds me that there is much in my life for which I am *thankful*, and gives me confidence as I bring my *supplications* to God. By "Praying the Scriptures" the pressure is no longer on me to set the agenda. My task is to listen and respond prayerfully to a gracious and loving God.

A second way of using Scripture as the foundation for our prayer life dates back to the sixth century when St. Benedict established the basic form of "spiritual reading" (*lectio divina*).[13] This approach is based on the biblical concept that the faithful person is to meditate on God's word (Ps. 1:1-2), and it was used and strongly advocated by well-known Protestant leaders, such as John Calvin and Richard Baxter.

In this method of using the Bible when we pray, an essential assumption is that there are two ways to read. We can either read to gain "information," which is the way we usually approach a newspaper; or we can read for "formation," which is the way we read personal letters from friends and family members. To approach Scripture to gain information is fine, but that is not the thrust behind God's word. Through the Bible God desires to form a relationship with us, not merely pass on information to us. In order to facilitate this formative activity, spiritual reading employs four phases: reading, meditation, prayer, and contemplation.

In the first phase, one reads (*lectio*) the biblical passage. In particular, one must first read slowly and reflectively. One is not rushing to cover as much material as possible in order to glean shallow information. The goal is to read slowly, expecting that God will draw your attention to a key aspect of the passage, something that will encourage or convict you. The question to ask yourself as you begin is "God, what are you saying to me just now?"[14]

The second phase is meditation (*meditatio*), and we must not be confused about this step. Here the goal is not, as in Eastern meditation, an emptying of one's thoughts. Rather, the Christian approach to meditation is an active interaction with the thoughts which God and Scripture place in our minds. Where do our lives intersect with the biblical passage? For example, if you were reading Mark 2:1ff., where four people remove a roof so as to take their crippled friend to Jesus for healing, what would you think if you were there? With which character would you identify? Would it be the cripple's desperation? His friends' hope? The scribes' anger? The crowd's confusion? Why would you respond as you do? What is currently at work in your own life that would lead you to respond to the story in this way? What would Jesus say to you given your response?

The next step is spoken prayer (*oratio*). Our time of meditation on the biblical text will certainly provide a subject or subjects about which to pray. Who would not want to offer prayers of gratitude to Christ who accepts and heals us when we turn to him in our weakness? Clearly confessions and prayers of repentance are called for when we find ourselves angry and offended by God's work. This third phase of the process "allows for a full range of human response to tumble forth in heart-felt prayer to the One for whom we were made."[15]

Finally, we move to contemplation (*contemplatio*). Once we have entered into genuine prayer with God we simply rest in God's presence. We need do nothing but keep silent and be ready to receive whatever God may want to do. We sit waiting for God to speak. There is nothing more for us to do but wait expecting God to continue the conversation.

At this point, the question arises: how long does this take? This is no quick breezing through a biblical passage and then getting on with our lives. One should plan on a minimum of thirty minutes of silent distraction-free time to develop this formative prayer approach. And it will take practice. But remember God, through the Holy Spirit, is always with us and always desirous to communicate with us in the hope that we will be formed into his Son's image.

Talking to God

If the goal of prayer is transformed lives, it should be clear that we must move beyond one direction (human to God) conversations or placing others at the center of our prayers. To view prayer primarily as petition or our "telling" God the status of our needs and concerns misses the crucial point that God wants to speak to us about the divine agenda for our lives. To intercede only for others, essentially amounts to gently pushing our friends and family members into God's presence, while we either lurk behind them or dash away. The core of real prayer is to move ourselves into God's presence and stay there waiting and listening for God's direction.

However, I would present a very one-sided view of living prayer-fully if I were to stop at this point, discussing only the importance of facilitating God's addressing us. If prayer is a genuine path to intimacy with God, there must be options for our addressing God.[16] The Bible assumes this, and the countless characters in Scripture repeatedly talk to God under every imaginable circumstance. Moses intercedes for the rebellious Israelites (Num. 14:13-25), Job cries out when overwhelmed with intense pain and suffering (i.e., Job 6–7), and Habakkuk vents his frustration over the way God works in the world (Hab.1:2-14). Even Jesus, though divine himself, found speaking to his Father an absolutely essential aspect of his life here on earth (i.e., Matt. 26:36-46; John 17). While this idea of talking to God has been partially addressed in the discussion of spoken prayer (*oratio*) above, I want to make two more specific points here.

First, when we do offer prayers to God, it seems absolutely crucial that we pray "from the heart." That is to say we cannot pray authentically if we pray without honesty. If we are overwhelmed by the depth of God's grace and love, then we should attempt to reflect that in our prayers. If we are angry and confused, we need to say that as best we can. If we are near despair, it does us no good to pretend we are not near the "edge." God will not be offended by our heart-felt honesty because, as noted in the first section of this chapter, we have an intercessor who interprets our genuine and yet flawed prayers to God. Jesus Christ sits at God's side clarifying our words and groans to God, just as he mediated God's words to us as we wait prayerfully.

A second point is that we need to learn to pray habitually throughout the course of our day. Acts of prayer cannot be limited to fifteen or thirty minutes at the start or end of the day. If we are to develop a truly intimate life with God, we must constantly condition ourselves to be prayerfully attuned to our need for God's presence in our world. One approach to praying this way involves what Richard Foster calls "simple prayer."[17] There are no "correct" words or formulas to be included in simple prayer. There is no way to pray "just right." As a matter of fact, if we think there is one proper way to pray, the chances are very good we will not develop intimate levels of prayer. And as Foster notes, the search for "just right" prayers says more about us as over-achievers than it does about God's sense of order.[18] God wants to hear our simple and straightforward prayers because they reveal who we are and the nature of our concerns. These prayers are quite simply prayers consisting of a few words or sentences. With this basic prayer form "we simply and unpreten-tiously share our concerns and make our petitions."[19]

One way in which we can offer simple prayers to God is through "praying the ordinary."[20] The assumption is that any "ordinary" experience can be used as an occasion for prayer, and we then consciously learn to invite God's presence into the mundane transactions of our lives. If we desire to develop prayer as a daily habit, we must see these normal events as opportunities for prayer and talking to God. Foster goes so far as to suggest "if we cannot find God in the routines of home and shop, then we will not find God at all."[21] Such an approach to prayer reminds us that God is interested in every minute of our lives, not just the minutes we devote to worship, Bible study, or formally structured prayer. Therefore, at work we can offer simple prayers for situations involving tense relationships or company deadlines. We can pray for news items we hear reported on the television or in the newspapers. We can pray for the reckless driver's protection (and hopefully change of driving habits) rather than comment on his stupidity. We can pray for our neighbors and their struggles. The prayer opportunities provided by our attention to the ebbs and flows of life are limitless. And to begin praying for these items is to begin praying without ceasing as Paul directs at various points in his letters (i.e., Rom.12:12; Eph. 6:18; Col. 4:2; 1 Thess. 5:17).

Once we develop approaches to prayer which highlight God speaking to us and honest, simple and frequent prayers from us, our common and traditional approach to prayer—petition and intercession—will take on new depth. If we have established an intimate prayer relationship with God, we will have confidence to ask knowing that we ask as wisely as we can, given what we have learned of God through our prayers. Certainly one crucial truth we will learn is that God loves us and wants only the best for us. Having established this theological truth in our hearts and minds, we will intercede for others and make our petitions with a "long view." As Majorie Thompson writes, "We can be confident that grace will be given in a way that best expresses God's loving purpose, with which we are united. It may take time for the grace to become manifest, and perseverance is commended (Luke 18:1-18)."[22] But God will hear, just as we have heard and have been promised.

Conclusion

There can be no doubt that we are called to lives which we cannot live through our own efforts. Equally, there is no doubt that we are not asked to rely on ourselves. God offers us an intimate relationship with himself through the work of Jesus Christ and his presence through the Holy Spirit. God encourages us to pray and change, primarily through listening but also through offering our ordinary and heart-felt concerns to him. When we begin to pray this way we will conclude

> Lord, I just don't understand
> this strange creature you call man.
> Who thinks he lives by his own
> hand, but I know
> There's no life away from you.[23]

Discussion Questions

1. Why is Jesus the focus as we consider relying on God? What does this mean for us?

2. In what ways can Jesus' continual mediation between us and God impact our prayers and Christian living? Would the influence be all beneficial or might there be negative implications?

3. Is this chapter's strong emphasis on prayer as spiritual formation and personal change too one-sided? Why or why not? Does prayer primarily change God or us?

4. This chapter makes the point that busyness is a serious challenge to "living prayerfully." What can we do to change this overactive aspect of our lifestyles?

5. What are other impediments you find in your prayer life in general? Specifically, how has fear held you back from experiencing all you can with God? How can fear and these other barriers be overcome?

6. Why should we want to be open to listening to God as part of our prayer life? What might this require of us? How ought we balance "listening" and "talking" when we pray?

7. As you understand both "praying the Bible" and "spiritual reading," would you pray these ways? Why or why not?

8. Why do we often try to conceal our deepest thoughts and feelings when we pray? Given biblical examples like Job and Habakkuk, how can we learn to talk to God more honestly?

9. Write or tell of a time when prayer was intimate and "two way." Share this with another person in the group.

10. Does this chapter's approach to prayer strike you as too "thought oriented?" What does a good balance between thoughtfulness and feelings look like with regard to one's prayer life?

For Further Reading

Guyon, Jeanne. *Experiencing the Depths of Jesus Christ.* Library of Spiritual Classics, vol. 2. Sargent, Cal.: SeedSowers Christian Books, 1975.

Johnson, Ben Campbell. *Listening for God.* Mahwah, N.J.: Paulist Press, 1997.

Johnson, Ben Campbell. *To Will God's Will: Beginning the Journey.* Philadelphia: Westminster Press, 1987.

Merton, Thomas. *Contemplative Prayer.* Garden City, N.J.: Image Books, 1971.

Nouwen, Henri J.M. *With Open Hands.* Notre Dame, Ind.: Ave Maria Press, 1995.

Endnotes

Introduction

[1]Aubrey Malphurs, *Value-Driven Leadership: Discovering and Developing Your Core Values for Ministry* (Grand Rapids, Mich.: Baker Book House, 1996), p. 11.

[2]Quoted in George Carey, *I Believe* (London: SPCK, 1991), p. 148.

[3]E. Morris Sider, *Reflections on a Heritage: Defining the Brethren in Christ.* (Nappanee, Ind.: The Brethren in Christ Historical Society and Evangel Press, 1999).

Chapter 1

[1]Philip Yancey, *What's So Amazing About Grace?* (Grand Rapids, Mich.: Zondervan Publishing House, 1997), p. 70.

Chapter 2

[1]*Effective Christian Education: A National Study of Protestant Congregations* included 11,000 members of 561 congregations in six United States Protestant denominations: Christian Church (Disciples of Christ), Evangelical Lutheran Church in America, United Presbyterian Church (U.S.A.), Southern Baptist Convention, United Church of Christ, and United Methodist. For more information on the study, contact Search Institute at 1-800-888-7828.

[2]Sara P. Little, "Rethinking Adult Education," in David S. Shuller, ed., *Rethinking Christian Education: Explorations in Theory and Practice* (St. Louis: Chalice Press, 1993), p. 101.

[3]George Gallup, Jr. and Robert Bezilla, *The Role of the Bible in American Society: On the Occasion of the 50th Anniversary of National Bible Week*, November 18-25, 1990 (Princeton, N.J.: Princeton Religion Research Center, 1990), p. 1.

[4]William F. Arndt and F. Wilbur Gingrich, *A Greek-English Lexicon of the New Testament and Other Early Christian Literature* (Chicago: The University of Chicago Press, 1957), pp. 91-92.

[5]See, as examples, the following references: Jesus' messiahship (Matt. 16:17); eternal life and the love of God (1 John 1:2-3; 4:9); the mystery of Christ (Gal. 1:16; Col. 1:25-26; 1 Tim. 3:16; Titus 1:3); and the wisdom and righteousness of God (Rom. 1:17; 2:9-10; Eph. 3:5-6).

[6]Arndt and Gingrich, pp. 277-278.

[7]Gallup and Bezilla, pp. 17-20.

[8]George Gallup, Jr. and Jim Castelli, *The People's Religion: American Faith in the '90s* (New York: Macmillan Publishing Company, 1989), p. 60.

[9]Benton Johnson, Dean R. Hoge, and Donald A. Luidens, "Mainline Churches: The Real Reason for Decline," *First Things* (March 1993), pp. 14-15.

[10]Johnson, Hoge, and Luidens, p. 18.

[11]The story is recorded in William J. Bausch, *Storytelling: Imagination and Faith* (Mystic, Conn.: Twenty-Third Publications, 1989), pp. 204-205.

[12]Ibid, p. 204.

[13]On the distinction between meaning and significance as related to the Bible, see Perry B. Yoder, *Toward Understanding the Bible* (Newton, Kan.: Faith and Life Press, 1978).

Chapter 3

[1]G.I. Williamson, *The Shorter Catechism* (Phillipsburg, N.J.: Presbyterian and Reformed Publishing Co., 1970).

Chapter 4

[1]Dallas Willard, *The Divine Conspiracy* (San Francisco: HarperSanFrancisco, 1998), p. 275.

[2]Bruce Wilkinson, *First Hand Faith* (Sisters, Ore.: Multnomah Publishers, 1996), p. 51.

[3]Editorial, "Make Disciples, Not Just Converts," *Christianity Today* (October 25, 1999), p. 29.

[4]Mark Buchanan, "Trapped in the Cult of the Next Thing," *Christianity Today* (September 6, 1999), p. 64.

[5]Willard, p. 275.

[6]Dietrich Bonhoeffer, *The Cost of Discipleship* (New York: Macmillan, 1953), p. 84.

[7]Ibid., p. 51.

Chapter 5

[1]Leonard Sweet, *Soul Tsunami* (Grand Rapids, Mich.: Zondervan, 1999), p. 220.

[2]Henri Nouwen, quoted in *Christianity Today* 40:6 (May 20, 1996), p. 80.

[3]Gordon Fee, *Paul's Letter to the Philippians* (Grand Rapids, Mich.: Eerdmans, 1995), p. 235.

[4]John Havlik, *People Centered Evangelism* (Nashville: Broadman Press, 1971), p. 47.

[5]Thomas Merton, quoted in *Christianity Today* 41:10 (September 1, 1997), p. 62.

[6]Bill Hybels, Easter sermon preached on April 12, 1998 (Tape #M9815).

[7]Fred Craddock, "When the Roll is Called Down Here," *Preaching Today*, #50.

Chapter 6

[1]Bill Hybels and Mark Mittelberg, *Becoming a Contagious Christian* (Grand Rapids, Mich.: Zondervan, 1994), p. 22.

[2]David Hall, "Brethren in Christ Core Values: Witnessing to the World" (sermon preached at the Elizabethtown Brethren in Christ Church, October 17, 1999), p. 3.

[3]Warren Hoffman, *Secret of the Harvest* (Nappanee, Ind.: Evangel Press, 1988), p. 105.

[4]George Gallup, Jr., "Secularism & Religion: Trends in Contemporary America," *Emerging Trends* 9 (December 1987), p. 3.

[5]Kenneth Latourette, "The First Five Centuries," p. 117, as quoted in *Evangelism in the Early Church*, Michael Green (Grand Rapids, Mich.: Eerdmans Publishing Company, 1970), p. 203.

[6]Rebecca Pippert, *Out of the Saltshaker and into the World* (Downers Grove, Ill.: InterVarsity Press, 1979).

[7]Leighton Ford, *The Christian Persuaders* (Downers Grove, Ill.: InterVarsity Press, 1976), p. 20.

[8]Joe Aldrich, *Life-Style Evangelism* (Portland, Ore.: Multnomah Press, 1981), p. 29.

[9]Michael Green, *Evangelism in the Early Church* (Grand Rapids, Mich.: Eerdmans Publishing Company, 1970), p. 194.

[10]Aldrich, p. 83.

[11]Bill Hybels, *Honest to God* (Grand Rapids, Mich.: Zondervan Publishing House, 1990), p. 126.

[12]Aldrich, p. 133.

[13]Christian Schwarz, *Natural Church Development* (Carol Stream, Ill.: Church Smart Resources, 1996), p. 69.

[14]Patrick Johnson, *The Church is Bigger Than You Think* (Bucks, Great Britain: WEC, 1998), pp. 97-116.

Chapter 7

[1]A similar learning experience occurs in Luke 10. After telling the parable of the Good Samaritan, Jesus discusses its implications with the inquiring lawyer: "'Which of these three, do you think, was a neighbor to the man who fell into the hands of the robbers?' He (the lawyer) said, 'The one who showed him mercy.' Jesus said to him, 'Go and do likewise'" (vv. 36-37).

[2]This harmony is demonstrated, among other ways, in the naming of the animals (2:19-20). In the Old Testament, names are important and carry meaning—they reflect the unique character of the one being named. Therefore, rather than constituting a simple exercise in typing or categorizing, naming the animals involved an intimate and experiential knowledge on humanity's part (cf. Gen. 3:20; 17:5, 15; John 1:42, 47-48; Rev. 2:17).

[3]Both the female, who was deceived (cf. 2 Cor. 11:3), and the male, who acted in full knowledge with his partner, chose to rebel against God and throw off their role as rulers under God. Thus, through their disobedience, they cast aside the place of service before God in an attempt to gain equality with God.

[4]James N. Churchyard, "The French and Indian Raid on Deerfield, Massachusetts, 1704," *http://www.crossmyt.com/hc/gen/derrfild.html*.

[5]"The Pia Desideria," *Christian History* V:2 (1986), p. 30.

[6]Thomas Merton, *New Seeds of Contemplation* (New York: New Directions, 1962), p. 83.

[7]Andrew Purvis, "Mourning the Angels of Mercy," *TIME* 145:22 (May 29, 1995).

[8]Thomas à Kempis, *The Imitation of Christ* (Uhrichsville, Ohio: Barbour and Company, 1984 [Reprint ed.]), Third Book, Chapter X, No. 5.

[9]Howard Snyder, *Community of the King* (Downers Grove, Ill.: InterVarsity Press, 1978), p. 190.

[10]In the words of Dietrich Bonhoeffer, "When Christ calls a man, He bids him come and die." *The Cost of Discipleship* (New York: Simon and Schuster, 1995 [Reprint ed.]), p. 9.

[11]Carlton Wittlinger, *Quest for Piety and Obedience* (Nappanee, Ind.: Evangel Press, 1978), p. 163.

[12] See, as examples, John 13:3-35; Acts 2:44-46; 4:32-35; Galatians 5:13; and 1 John 3:16-18.

[13]Such acts of service might include driving people in need of transportation to church or the grocery store, loaning money without interest, providing meals for others in distress, or mowing lawns for the elderly or disabled. For a related discussion, see Richard Foster, *Celebration of Discipline* (San Francisco: Harper & Row, 1978), pp. 110-122.

[14]Quoted in "Perspectives 96," *Newsweek* (December 30, 1996), p. 127.

[15]See Donald Dayton, *Discovering an Evangelical Heritage* (New York: Harper & Row, 1976), p. 119.

Chapter 8

[1]A number of words have been used over the years to describe how we make peace, both within the church and in society. Some of these words are nonresistance (coming from Matt. 5:39, "Do not resist an evildoer"), pacifism, and nonviolence. The words connote different things to different people, resulting in preferences for one word over another. In this essay, regardless of the word used, I am assuming a common commitment to a pursuit of peace that promotes alternatives to war and physical violence.

[2]E. J. Swalm. *Nonresistance Under Test* (Nappanee, Ind.: E. V. Publishing House, 1939).

[3]Gwen White, "An Unlikely Journey," *Evangelical Visitor* (January 1991), pp. 9-10.

[4]"Confession of Faith of the Brethren," reprinted in C.O. Wittlinger, *Quest for Piety and Obedience: The Story of the Brethren in Christ* (Nappanee, Ind.: Evangel Press, 1978), p. 554.

[5]"Articles of Faith and Doctrine," *Manual of Doctrine and Government of the Brethren in Christ Church* (Nappanee, Ind.: Evangel Publishing House, 1998), p. 17. The complete paragraph, within the section entitled "Mission of the Church: In Relation to the World," reads thus: "Christ loved his enemies and He calls us as His disciples to love our enemies. We follow our Lord in being a people of peace and reconciliation, called to suffer and not to fight. While respecting those who hold other interpretations, we believe that preparation for or participation in war is inconsistent with the teachings of Christ. Similarly, we reject all other acts of violence which devalue human life. Rather, we affirm active peacemaking, sacrificial service to others, as well as the pursuit of justice for the poor and oppressed in the name of Christ."

[6]Cited in John Driver, *How Christians Made Peace with War* (Scottdale, Pa.: Herald Press, 1988), p. 26.

Chapter 9

[1]Quoted in Kathleen Norris, *The Cloister Walk* (New York: Riverhead Books, 1996), p. 328.

[2]See, for example, *Saturday Night* 111:3 (April 1996), p. 19; *Harvard Health Letter* 22:10 (August 1997), pp. 1-3; and *FDA Consumer* (July/August 1998).

[3]Tom Sine, *Mustard Seed vs. McWorld* (Grand Rapids, Mich.: Baker Books, 1999), p. 81.

[4]Quoted in *Discipleship Journal* (Issue 112), p. 40.

Chapter 10

[1]Henri J.M. Nouwen, *With Open Hands* (Notre Dame, Ind.: Ave Maria Press, 1995), p. 79.

[2]James B. Torrance, *Worship, Community, and the Triune God of Grace* (Downers Grove, Ill.: InterVarsity Press, 1996), p. 44.

[3]Ibid., pp. 45-46.

[4]*Celebration of Discipline: The Path to Spiritual Growth,* 20th Anniversary Edition (San Francisco, Calif.: HarperSanFrancisco, 1998), p. 33.

[5]*The Path of Waiting* (New York, NY: Crossroads, 1995), p. 6.

[6]*With Open Hands*, p. 11.

[7]A very helpful and general writing on prayer can be found in Marjorie J. Thompson's *Soul Feast: An Invitation to the Christian Spiritual Life* (Louisville, Ky.: Westminster John Knox Press, 1995), pp. 31-51.

[8]Library of Spiritual Classics, Volume 2 (Sargent, Ga.: SeedSowers Christian Books Publishing House, 1975).

[9]Ibid., pp. 144-145.

[10]Ibid., p. 8.

[11]Ibid., p. 9.

[12]George Carey, *I Believe* (London: SPCK, 1991), p. 61.

[13]Much of what follows is gleaned from chapter 2 of Marjorie Thompson's text cited in note 7. A very fine introduction to this prayer form by an evangelical writer is Jan Johnson's *Listening to God* (Colorado Springs, Co.: NavPress Publishing, 1998). Johnson's text includes numerous useful outlines for *lectio divina* sessions for both individuals and groups.

[14]Thompson, p. 23.

[15]Ibid., p. 24.

[16]A good place to begin exploring the complexity of our role in prayer is Richard Foster's *Prayer* (San Francisco, Calif.: HarperSanFrancisco, 1992).

[17]Ibid., pp. 7-15.

[18]Ibid., p. 7.

[19]Ibid., p. 9.

[20]Ibid., pp. 169-178.

[21]Ibid., p. 171.

[22]Thompson, p. 23.

[23]Matt Morginsky, "Away from You," *Chase the Sun*, BEC Recordings #140-20.